a Horse in the Suburbs

Drawings on pages 43, 53, 90, 93, 96, 109, 112, and 119, Karl Stuecklen.

Photographs: Page 4, British Columbia Government Photograph. Page 23, State Historical Society of Wisconsin. Pages 27 and 137, Kentucky Department of Public Information. Page 47, Rick Smith. Page 99, Grant Heilman. Frontispiece and pages 10, 12, 18, 20, 28, 34, 39, 55, 58, 60, 66, 68, 70, 77, 84, 87, 89, 97, 101, 105, 123, 130, 133, and 142, Liz Rogers.

This book has been produced in the United States of America. It is designed by R. L. Dothard Associates and is published by The Stephen Greene Press, Brattleboro, Vermont 05301.

Library of Congress Cataloging in Publication Data

Davis, Lloyd H.   1919-
  Keeping a horse in the suburbs.

  Bibliography: p.
  1. Horses.   I.   Title.
SF285.3.D38   636.1   76-13808
ISBN 0-8289-0285-2

77   78   79   80   9   8   7   6   5   4   3   2

Contents

Foreword, 7

1 Do You Really Want a Horse? 11

The bright side: enjoyment and education. Recreation. Caution: work and repairs. Hazards and liability. Boarding your horse. Expenses.

2 The Popularity of Horses, 22

"Horse power" in the past. The horse makes a comeback.

3 Buying a Horse, 30

A horse for your needs. Breeds. A pony for the children? Horse characteristics: size, age, sex, color, condition, disposition, performance. Cost. Horse trading. Where to buy a horse.

4 Horse Sense: Knowing and Handling Your Horse, 50

The horse's senses. Moods and emotions. Motivation. The psychology of training. Loading a horse into a trailer. Catching a runaway.

5 Horse Care, 69

Nutrition: pasture, hay, feed supplements, water. Parasite control. Disease control. Preventive medicine. Grooming. Hoof care. Putting a horse down.

6 Horse Equipment, 92

Saddles. Bits and bridles. Halters and other equipment. Buying a trailer.

7 Sensible Facilities for Your Horse, 104

Natural and suburban environments. Shelter and storage facilities. Feeding facilities. Clean water. Pasture. Fences. Secure gates.

8 Pasture and Stable Maintenance, 120

Pasture management. Using stable space wisely. Controlling flies. Controlling rodents. Manure disposal.

9 The Horseman and the Community, 129

Community events: shows, horse clubs, youth programs. Cooperative action. Community relations. Trail-riding. Horsemen's organizations.

10 How to Find Out More, 139

Other sources of information. A note on safety. Enjoyment.

Appendix, 143

Glossary, 143; Bibliography, 146; State Horse Councils, 147; Horsemen's Organizations, 149; State Extension Specialists, 150; Magazines for Horsemen, 152; Breed Registries, 155; National Parks and Forests with Bridle Trails, 158.

Index, 161

Foreword

Today about half a million families own one to three horses, and thousands of others with small acreages in urban, suburban, or rural areas would like to own horses. Many people have had little previous experience in horse ownership. If you are one of them, this book is intended to help you. Owning and using a horse can be very enjoyable, educational, and satisfying for old and young alike. Or it can be dangerous, confining, and a community nuisance. The purpose of this book is to help horse ownership provide satisfaction and joy and to help those who have or would have a horse avoid problems and pitfalls that could turn a good hobby into a bore.

This book is born of the inadequacies of existing books, many of which seem to assume the horse owner lives in wide open spaces and is familiar with horses and the special language of horse people. If a book could be said to have parents, this one's parents would be the need for knowledge by many newcomers to horse ownership who have little land, and the need to present that knowledge in a clear and simple way.

I've written this book from the point of view of one who has kept, used, and enjoyed horses for many years in the suburbs of a large metropolitan area. I've drawn on my own experiences and those of my friends and neighbors, as well as on my background of farm life and agricultural science.

This book does not cover all that could be discussed, but I have selected those subjects that my experience indicates are of primary importance to my audience and are not properly treated in other popular publications. However, so the reader can obtain more detailed knowledge on specialized subjects, a bibliography of suggested references is included in the Appendix.

L. H. D.
Great Falls, Virginia
Summer 1976

Keeping a Horse in the Suburbs

♞ 1
Do you really want a horse?

The bright side: enjoyment and education

There are many reasons for wanting a horse.

For the old and young in your family the horse will provide enjoyable and invigorating recreation. It can be the key that opens the door to lasting friendships, and it can help you build a positive role in your community.

For the young people in your family, the horse will have special educational value. Caring for the horse will develop a sense of responsibility and bring satisfaction from their accomplishments. Through the horse, they will learn about nutrition of animals, disease prevention and control, physiology, and (believe it or not) the psychology of getting along with people.

When you get a horse, someone will have to take care of him—at least feed and water him twice a day. If this is your daughter's responsibility, for example, and she is late, the horse may whinny and stamp in annoyance. He also will let her know that he appreciates her attention. A young person almost invariably responds by accepting her new responsibility. Your daughter will want her friend, the horse, to be well fed and healthy. She will be anxious to learn about nutrition and parasites. When the horse is sick or hurt she will take care of him. Before long you have a new member of the family.

You will find great inner satisfaction in observing the relationship between your child and the horse as the horse stands by the fence while she strokes his mane, or the two of them take off over the countryside, her eyes shining with pride and enthusiasm. (If things don't start going this way, perhaps you need to re-evaluate the situation.)

It will not take long to learn that a horse has a mind of its own. To get her horse to do her bidding, your daughter will want to know how the horse thinks. She will learn to use punishment, rewards, praise, and rebuke to make her relationship with the horse more satisfying. And later, she will discover that the mind of the horse and the mind of a human have much in common, and she will find ways to use these lessons to improve her relationships with people.

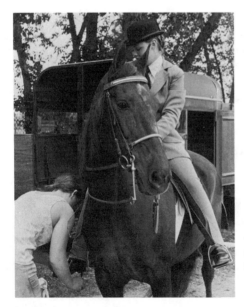

Final spit and polish before an event at a Massachusetts Morgan Club show. Horses are judged on conformation, action, and manners.

Caring for and riding a horse is one way children can develop an appreciation of nature and respect and affection for all of God's creatures. They will develop skills they can enjoy all of their lives. And the experiences they have are likely to spark interests that may set afire an enthusiasm for a lifelong career. One of the most common vocational interests awakened by the horse experience is veterinary medicine. Many veterinarians developed their first interest in the profession by owning a horse. But the experiences related to keeping a horse are varied and lead to a great diversity of vocational interests. My son, who loves trail-riding in the wilderness, developed a keen interest in ecology and finally studied landscape architecture. Others have been led by their horses into human medicine, psychology, nutrition, and a variety of scientific fields.

Recreation on horseback

You may just want a horse to ride in the countryside. The value of such a ride can't be fully appreciated until you come home from work some spring evening filled with the tensions of a job, saddle up the old mare, and ride off through the solitude of the fields and forests. No other way does nature seem so sweet or spring flowers appear so beautiful. It is great therapy for the human soul—and good exercise, if you live a sedentary life.

You may prefer human companionship to solitude. If so, there probably is a riding club in your community, or certainly other people with a like interest. Trotting down the trails with your neighbor will lead to experiences you will want to relive together and to strong bonds of friendship.

You may become a horse-show enthusiast. Shows offer the opportunities to display your skill as a horseman, show off the beauty and ability of your horse, and feel the excitement of competition. And a shelf full of ribbons and trophies is a constant reminder of past accomplishments.

There are many types of shows, such as local shows conducted mainly for enjoyment by people in the community, shows for horses of a specific breed, and shows for English riding or Western riding. You can compete in your immediate area or on a national scale. It can be an occasional thing, occupy most of your weekends, or become an almost full-time activity. If you want to learn more about shows and what they have to offer, contact the American Horse Shows Association—a national organization that provides a variety of services to people conducting horse shows (see Appendix for the address). Of course there are plenty of show enthusiasts in your community who will be glad to tell you about local events and encourage you to participate.

Rodeos provide an exciting form of competition especially in certain parts of the country, as does fox hunting in other areas. For more information about these events you can contact organizations in these fields (see Appendix for names and addresses).

Competitive trail-rides and endurance rides are new to some areas and growing in popularity among old and young horsemen alike. In these events participants ride long distances, up to 100 miles, in as short a time as one day. Special conditioning of horse and rider is essential. Judging is based on performance and on the condition of the horse throughout the race. There are organizations that can tell you more about these events too (see Appendix).

Nearly every community has youth horse clubs. Participation in such clubs may be your reason for interest in getting a horse in the first place, for the clubs provide an excellent means of capitalizing on the many educational features of horse ownership. The club leaders are usually well-informed horsemen dedicated to passing their knowledge and skill on to young people.

You may want a horse because of a desire to participate in

any of these or other forms of horse recreation. As you get acquainted with other horsemen and learn about other activities in your area, your enjoyment of your horse will increase.

Caution: work and repairs

But what about the other side of the story? Let's take off the rose-colored glasses and look at some other considerations while you decide if you really want a horse.

A horse must have feed and water 365 days a year. If you are going to keep a horse at home, this can be confining to you. If you go for a Sunday picnic, you'll have to hurry home to feed the horse. How will you ever go away for a weekend or take a month's vacation?

This really shouldn't stand in your way if you plan ahead. Your horse-owning friends have the same problem. Perhaps you can take care of a friend's horse when he is away on the condition that he will do the same for you. Another solution, if you have the space, is to board a friend's horse and let the friend work off part of the cost by taking care of the horses once in a while. Then you have a worker with a personal interest in doing the job right. My family has been away for as long as a month at a time with this kind of arrangement.

There always is work to be done—feeding, hauling supplies, watering, cleaning stalls and paddocks, fixing fences, repairing the stable, mowing weeds, disposing of manure. There are jobs that strain some muscles, some that are less than pleasant—and a few that are downright obnoxious.

Throughout this book we suggest ways to handle these chores and make the work less of a burden. You can organize so that the necessary work will take only a few minutes a day to care for three or four horses, and you can keep horses without creating a community nuisance.

Hazards and liability

Will a horse in a residential area be a hazard to children? Maybe so. You can expect all the kids in the neighborhood to hang on your fence petting the horse and pulling grass to feed him. Indeed, some of the children may climb into the paddock or stable to pet the horse. These situations can be serious problems and should not be overlooked by a person keeping a horse in a suburban environment.

Above all, in such a situation, don't keep a horse who has shown any inclination to bite people or kick at them. Avoid the mean or vicious horse, regardless of his good qualities.

But even the most gentle horse may kick when startled or can step on someone's foot unintentionally. To avoid this, have a good fence and gates that are not easily opened by small children (see Chapter 7). Whenever you see a child entering the pasture, send him out. Be sure other parents in the neighborhood know the hazards and are always on the lookout. Perhaps the easiest way to avoid problems is to spend a little time catering to the children's interest: help them feed the horses and pet them where it is safe, and warn them of the dangers.

The children in your community will want to ride your horse. They may say they know how to ride. (It seems that everyone who has ever seen a Western movie thinks he can get on and gallop off into the sunset without training.) You might have an old horse well-schooled in training young riders, but the odds are you don't. More likely your horse will be startled or confused by the antics of a greenhorn, and you can't tell what he may do—run, buck, or just stand still.

You better have a firm rule for handling these situations and stick with it. As a minimum, check out the riding skill of kids who want to ride. If they pass your test you may want to get permission from their parents. If they are going to ride, check your insurance policy to be sure your liability is covered.

Boarding your horse

Will the horse odors create a community nuisance, and will a paddock be unsightly? It's a possibility. One way to avoid some of these problems and keep peace in the neighborhood is to board your horse. (Of course, if you board your horse, the young people in your family will not fully benefit from the educational value of keeping a horse.)

If you look around you will find places near by where boarding horses is a business. Also, there are people who have a horse or two and welcome the opportunity to board another to help pay their bills. They may also ask you to help take care of the horses when they are away. How do you find them? Look in the want ads of the Sunday paper, ask other people who have horses, or just drive the roads and knock on doors of places with horses.

A word of caution: you may find that the kind of care and treatment horses receive at boarding establishments varies considerably. You want your horse to have the kind of treatment you would give him, so don't be afraid to ask questions about how they feed, handle, and care for their horses. Also observe the horses that are there. Do they seem well fed and healthy? Do they act as though they have been well treated? Are the premises clean? Hang around and talk with others who keep horses there and see if they are satisfied.

Boarding costs vary greatly, as do the services for which you pay. For example, you can find boarding establishments that provide an indoor riding arena for your use, keep the horses in stalls, clean the stalls daily, groom and exercise the horse daily, administer medicines for you as needed, supply any feed or feed supplements you may request, and provide additional services. Another place may keep the horses in a large pasture with a shed for protection from the weather, and may depend on you to administer medicines, groom your horse, and exercise him. Either set-up could be highly satisfactory, depending on your situation and your horse.

Horses await grain and grooming at a large boarding stable. Many stables also offer riding lessons to new horsemen.

I am reminded of the story of a person who was looking for a place to board a horse. He checked at several places. At one the fee was $100 a month. The proprietor fed, groomed, exercised, and doctored the horses, and he said the horse owner could have the manure. At another stable the fee was $20 and naturally the services were less. And there was no mention of manure. When asked about that, the proprietor replied, "At $20 a month there won't be any manure."

In horse boarding, as in other things, you tend to get what you pay for. Be sure your responsibilities and those of the boarding establishment are clearly spelled out. Here are some questions you may overlook:

How often do they clean stalls and drinking equipment? Will the horse be groomed? Will he be inspected regularly for injury and illness? Who calls the veterinarian when needed? Who pays him? Will medicines be administered? Will the horse receive special feeds you or the vet may prescribe? Who pays for them? What do they feed, and how often? How good is the hay? Will the horse be in a pasture or paddock with other horses of similar temperament? Should the horse have a blood test for "swamp fever"? Are new horses segregated for a few days to detect any contagious diseases?

Although costs will vary with services, you might obtain satisfactory pasture boarding for as little as $20 a month—or if you want everything, you can pay as much as $150 in some urban areas.

Some states and localities regulate horse boarding establishments to assure good horse care. You might check with your local SPCA (Society for the Prevention of Cruelty to Animals) about such regulations, and they might be able to recommend places they consider to be of high quality.

Facilities at home

If you plan to keep your horse at home, you will need some space and some facilities. In many suburban communities, local zoning ordinances frequently specify minimum requirements for horse facilities. You may also find restrictions in your deed applying to facilities and horse care. You will want to investigate them carefully and comply with them fully.

Ideally, a horse should be in as natural a situation as possible. He should have large areas in which to roam freely, with an abundance of grass and a readily available supply of fresh water. The more man compromises with this ideal, the more problems arise and the more provisions must be made to handle the problems. Within limits, these provisions can be made satisfactorily at low costs (see Chapter 7). In my experience, however, satisfactory measures are extremely difficult on a lot of one acre or less, and impractical in most suburban situations unless two acres or more are available.

Expenses

For most of us, one of the big factors affecting our answer to the question "Do you really want a horse?" is money. How much will it cost? That I cannot tell you easily, because it depends on many things. A horse can be a very expensive hobby or he can be managed on a very modest budget. It's the same old story—it's more the cost of high living than the high cost of living. And over the long run, it's not so much the initial expense as the upkeep.

If you hire someone to put up a fancy stable, build a high-cost fence, get a registered horse with an established show record, call the vet every time the horse coughs, go to a show every weekend, have the best new trailer with a high-cost hitch and powerful car to pull it, buy the latest in fancy riding apparel, get the very best tack, feed all the latest mineral and vitamin supplements as well as the more expensive feeds, participate fully in the hunt, throw frequent parties after the show or hunt—well, then you are considering a way of life, not just a hobby. And you'd better have the income to go with it.

On the other hand, all this is not necessary for a very enjoyable horse hobby. Throughout this book I'll give some ideas on ways you can keep costs down. The following table may provide a rough guide of what to expect; I'll explain the variations later.

INITIAL HORSE INVESTMENT

	MINIMUM (WITH BARN AND FENCES)	AVERAGE
Horse	$200	$500
Saddle, bridle, etc.	150 (used)	300
Special clothes for rider	–	75
Small stable	–	1,500
Board fences (to enclose 2 acres)	–	1,500
	$350	$3,875

ANNUAL COSTS, PER HORSE

	PROBABLE RANGE		
Feed and pasture management	$200	to	$ 500
Vet bills and medicines	50	to	200
Horseshoeing and hoof care	10	to	50
Special clothing for rider	20	to	100
Interest on investment	30	to	300
Depreciation: horse, buildings, fence	30	to	300
Fence and building repair	50	to	100
Horse transportation for one round trip, locally. (If you have a trailer, add license, depreciation, interest, and cost of pulling.)	40	to	50
	$430	to	$1,600

Your new lifestyle

If you do get a horse, there will be some changes in your life. Your whole family probably will fall in love with the animal. You and others in your family will become enthusiastic about horse-related activities, and you probably will find less time for golf or other activities of the past. Your old friends will start thinking you're a little "touched in the head." But there will be a host of new friends who suffer from the "malady" you have contracted and think you are quite normal.

2

The popularity of horses

One humorist observed that if Lady Godiva were to ride a horse through our city streets today it would cause quite a commotion—because so few people have seen a horse. While the humorist may have been knowledgeable about naked ladies, he certainly was not well informed about public interest in horses in our urban society. Horse-based recreation of all sorts is expanding rapidly in all parts of the country, particularly in large urban areas.

"Horse power" in the past

Until early in the twentieth century the people of our nation were almost entirely dependent on horses and mules for the power to perform a great many essential functions. The horse was an essential part of the daily lives of the people, who relied on this faithful servant in many ways.

In the city, horses pulled milk wagons, ice wagons, beer wagons, and coal wagons, delivering a multitude of products to urban consumers. Horses also drew the streetcars, taxis, and carriages that urban and rural people used for transportation. Teams of galloping horses pulled firemen and pumpers to fires, and in large cities policemen patrolled their beats on horseback.

On the farm, which everyone depended on for food, horses and mules moved the plows and other implements to till the soil. They pulled the early hay-making machines, and they hauled the produce to market in wagons and canalboats.

Horses pulled a steam pumper to a fire in Milwaukee in 1900. Rival fire companies often urged their horses to breakneck speeds, trying to be the first to "lay water" on a blaze.

In rural areas people were especially dependent on their horses. In many areas the doctor came on horseback, and the first rural mailmen used horses to deliver the mail. The horse-pulled carts of itinerant photographers and patent-medicine salesmen were familiar sights on country roads, and occasionally the brightly painted wagons of a traveling circus rumbled past, headed for the next town. Horse races and pulling contests provided exciting diversions. Children rode horses to school. A man's wealth was judged by the quality of his horses, and his character was known by the way he treated them.

In war, too, our nation depended on horses. Cavalry troops were elite mobile attack forces, and horses also pulled the cannon and supply wagons. Horses suffered and died with their masters in battle.

It is no wonder that we came to measure power in terms of "horse power," or that people came to believe that a horseshoe nailed over a door brought good luck. In such a world people said that a hard worker "works like a horse," that a person with good judgment had "horse sense," and that a strong-willed person was "stubborn as a mule." These and other horse-related expressions continue to be a part of the American language, reflecting the role of horses in our heritage.

As the population of our nation grew, so did the horse population. The livery stable was an indispensable feature of all towns and cities—serving in the role that Avis and Hertz play today. Large areas of farmland were devoted to producing hay and oats to feed the horses of the cities as well as those working on the farms.

But all this began to change with the invention of the internal combustion engine and its applications to transportation and power needs. Gradually tractors, trucks, cars, and other powered vehicles replaced the horse in most of the roles he had so faithfully performed, until today it is only in cattle ranching, a very few farm operations, certain forestry work, and other work on very rough terrain that we rely on horses for transportation and power.

This change has been a basic contribution to our national energy shortage. All work—all movement of people and things—requires energy from some source. The horse gets his energy from the grass, hay, and grain he eats—and these plants store energy they receive from the sun. The energy used by internal combustion engines comes from petroleum, energy from the sun stored millions of years ago. During the last century we have switched from hay and oats (renewable each year) to petroleum (nonrenewable) for much of our energy needs.

The switch from horses to mechanical power also affected our agricultural production, for at one time about 30 percent of the cropland of our farms was needed to produce feed for horses and mules. As we switched to petroleum for power this land was released to grow other things—a major factor in the expanding farm production of food and fiber during the last half century, needed to feed a growing population.

The number of horses on farms continued to increase until about 1915. At that time there were about twenty-eight million horses and mules on farms. We never did have a count of the horses faithfully performing city and other off-farm chores. No one knows how many horses there were in the United States when their numbers reached a peak, but it certainly was well over thirty million.

After about 1915 the number of horses started a long decline, and there seems to have been a corresponding declining public interest in matters having to do with the horse.

The low point in horse numbers probably was reached about 1950. At that time there were between two million and three million horses and mules on farms, and probably a few thousand in other places. The horse was all but gone from the American scene—and nearly forgotten. At that time one could travel hundreds of miles through the country and never see a horse, except for a few aging servants turned to pasture to live out their years. Large areas of farm country, once dependent on horses for many facets of human life, contained scarcely a horse.

Among the millions of people, ex-farm boys and others, whose daily work was made easier by substituting motor power for horse power, few tears were shed over the change.

The horse makes a comeback

Apparently it was in the early 1950's that the horse started his comeback and horse numbers began to increase. The growth was slow at first, speeding up as it went along. No one knows for sure how many horses there are in the country today (1976). There are at least eight and one-half million, and perhaps as many as ten million. The horse population has doubled since 1960, and is continuing its rapid increase throughout the 1970's.

Some indication of the rate of growth in horse numbers is provided by the number of new registrations in the purebred horse registries. Changes in these data represent changes in the number of births of purebred foals. The number of new registrations for the years 1960, 1968, and 1973 are available from thirteen purebred horse registries, accounting for nearly all of the purebred light horses. In those breeds new registrations were about 70,000 in 1960, 138,000 in 1968, and 191,000 in 1973—an increase of nearly 300 percent.

The Quarter Horse registry, the largest and fastest-growing equine registry, recorded 97,000 American Quarter Horses during 1975 alone. New registrations per year of Appaloosa went from 4,000 in 1960 to 20,000 in 1973. Among Arabians, another breed growing in popularity, new registrations per year went from 1,600 to 12,000 over the thirteen-year period. Half-Arabians went from 2,200 to 13,000 new registrations per year at the same time. Thoroughbreds increased from 13,000 per year in 1960 to 25,500 annually by 1973. (These statistics are from the American Horse Council.) While we do not have data on the total population of horses of these breeds, it is clear that these large increases in numbers of new registrations must result in a population explosion.

We have no statistics to reveal the increase in the number of grade horses, but most evidence indicates that the total horse population—grade and purebred—is rising rapidly.

Horse racing, America's favorite spectator sport, at Churchill Downs in Lexington, Kentucky—a Carnegie Hall for Thoroughbreds.

But even without statistics it is not difficult to observe the growing popularity of horses. As you travel through rural America you see horses in pastures everywhere. Drive the back roads of the suburbs around any city, and the number of white board fences, riding rings, and horse trailers in dooryards is impressive. Most communities have at least one tack shop—a service that probably was not there ten years ago.

In almost any suburban community there is at least one horse show per weekend during spring, summer, and fall, with the horse trailers making a procession on local streets. The American Horse Council estimates that there are 3,200,000 horse owners in the United States. And 107,000,000 people watched equine events in 1974, including horse races—America's most popular spectator sport.

Keeping and raising horses can involve every family member, and horses return their owners' affection in equal measure.

Every Fourth of July parade from Maine to California includes beautifully caparisoned horses and proud riders representing local horse clubs. In fact, some suburban communities with scarcely a full-time farmer have more horses than when the land was all in operating farms powered by horses.

The pleasure horse is back.

The rebirth of interest in horses probably is due to many things. The philosopher might observe that for thousands of years men and horses have been together. Man has depended on the horse for transportation and for power; men and horses have been close companions and partners in war and peace. He might conclude that such a relationship, so long established and so deeply imbedded in human experience, cannot be broken easily in one or two generations. He might even suggest that this interest in and affection for horses is deeply imbedded in the human personality and something close to instinctive. The economist might observe that a horse hobby probably is no more expensive, and perhaps less so, than golf, sailing, photography, or some other activity. Furthermore, you can enjoy your horse in small snatches of time—compared to a commitment of several hours of time once you tee off or set sail.

Others might conclude that the growing popularity of horses and horse-related activities are a part of a larger phenomenon—the return to nature and the simple life. Perhaps the people who flee the city for country living, who quit high-pressure jobs for more creative work, who grow food in their own gardens, who save to buy a piece of land, who lead the "ecology battle"—and those who love a horse—are responding to some basic human urge.

Or perhaps the horse trend is due in part to those people who manufacture and create a demand for attractive horse-related clothes, practical horse trailers, and so on. Another important factor is the excellent job that has been done by youth organizations in developing horse-related programs that appeal to young people and serve their needs.

No matter what the reason, every year thousands of additional families are owning and using horses. More and more suburban communities are providing space, facilities, and services for horsemen.

When you get down to basics, all of this is taking place because people enjoy it. They have found that they get great personal satisfaction from owning a horse. They have found pride in their accomplishments with the horse, they love the opportunities for communing with nature, they appreciate the educational experiences, and they enjoy the companionship with other horse lovers.

So why not follow your interest? Go ahead! Get a horse.

♞ 3
Buying a horse

Selecting a horse is a little like choosing a person to marry. Once made, the decision is hard to reverse. Disposing of a horse is about as difficult as disposing of a member of your family, once you and your family have developed an affection for the animal. Trading your horse in on another is likely to be a difficult and traumatic experience. You should be careful in selecting a horse to share your home, for you are likely to be committed to the decision for a long time.

A person gets great pride from his family and their accomplishments. Nothing gives parents greater pride than for people to remark that they have a beautiful and talented child. Your horse is a member of the family too, and you will get great satisfaction when people say, "You have a beautiful horse," or when your daughter, riding the horse in a community show, receives a fifth-place ribbon. As you buy a horse and must make compromises between your desires and your ability to pay, don't forget that you are acquiring another family member.

Selecting a horse for your needs

When you buy a machine or tool, you buy one suitable for the job you have to do. This principle should apply to buying a horse—especially if you are expecting very high levels of performance.

Horses vary in their body conformation and disposition. Horses with certain types of conformation have a natural ability to perform well in certain ways, just as superior basketball players are generally tall, or good wrestlers usually have a short, stocky build. Although most horses can do a variety of things, for superior performance in a specialized field you will want an animal with the conformation, disposition, and training for it. For instance, the draft breeds excel in pulling heavy loads, Thoroughbreds in racing, Quarter Horses in high speeds for short distances, Arabians in speed and endurance in covering great distances.

For example, if you want to start competing successfully in cutting-horse competition immediately, you should buy a horse who is trained, experienced, and has an established record as a winner. If you are not so anxious to win right away, you may be happy to pay a little less and buy one with conformation suitable for this use and with some winners in his ancestry. But you would not have high chances for success if you went to the track and bought an old Thoroughbred race horse to use as a cutting horse.

If you are interested in specialized competition and if you are willing to grow into your skill and performance ability along with your horse, get a horse with potential in that field rather than one who is an established champion. This is certain to save on your horse investment, and may give you greater satisfaction in the end.

Breeds of horses

Each breed has been developed through many generations of careful breeding, often for a special purpose. You should keep these special qualities in mind when you buy a horse.

The Arabian is the oldest breed, developed in the Arabian desert over many centuries to serve the needs of nomadic tribes. A man's horse was his means of survival, for it carried him across great expanses of desert in battle against enemy tribes. It was also his means of instant flight. The horse was a tribesman's most prized possession, a measure of his wealth, who shared with the family the security of their tent. In the desert environment horses developed great endurance, the ability to travel long distances at sustained high speeds. They were "easy keepers," horses that could survive and prosper on little feed. They were war horses with great courage, yet gentle companions in the family tent.

All registered Arabians today must trace all branches of their ancestry in official records back to the Arabian desert. Typically, an Arabian is small to middle-sized, with a short back, long arched neck, short head, broad forehead, and a tail carried high when he is in motion. As in his days in the desert, the Arabian today excels in his ability to travel long distances.

The Thoroughbred is a breed developed in Great Britain about two hundred years ago primarily for racing, by crossing Arabians with native breeds. Since then, the breed has been further developed for this specialized purpose. They are tall, long-legged horses with long necks.

Another horse bred primarily for racing is the American Quarter Horse. This breed originated in Virginia, where short, quarter-mile races were popular. The horses that could put on sudden bursts of speed to win these contests proved to be stocky horses with heavily muscled rear quarters—characteristic of the Quarter Horse today. From Virginia the Quarter Horse went west and became a popular working horse on cattle ranches, then spread back across the country as a pleasure horse, one of the most numerous and popular breeds today.

Tennessee Walking Horses were bred on plantations in the South to provide a smooth, easy ride for farmers who had to be in the saddle long hours every day. They continue to be prized for their special gaits and comfortable ride.

The Morgan was a New England development, a general-purpose horse who was expected to pull the plow, take the family to church in style, serve as a riding horse, and win races at the county fair. The Morgan is the only breed named after an individual horse—a stallion called Justin Morgan.

American Saddle Horses combine Thoroughbred and native blood to produce a riding horse that travels with a smooth gait and high action.

The Standardbred, another breed developed in America, has Thoroughbred and Arabian ancestors. Its specialty is racing while pulling a sulky. To win it must either trot or pace without breaking into a gallop.

The draft breeds are probably best known today because of the eight-horse team that represents a popular beer manufacturer. They are all large horses with heavy muscling over large-boned frames. Belgian, Percheron, and Clydesdale are the better known breeds. All were developed in Europe to carry knights heavily clad in armor and to do the world's heavy work before the days of gasoline engines.

These are but a few of the breeds and their traditional characteristics. You also will hear about "grade" horses: these are horses not known to be purebred, or horses having ancestors of two or more breeds. The term is used to refer to all horses that are not registered in any of the breed registries. A grade horse can be just as good in performance and disposition as a registered horse.

Most horses of the breeds commonly used for pleasure riding have the versatility that goes with being a good all-around athlete—more versatility than horse owners give them credit for. Most breeders of Morgans, Arabians, Quarter Horses, and American Saddle Horses, for instance, stress the versatility of their horses.

If a horse is sound and has good conformation and disposition, his abilities to serve you well in a variety of uses is limited more by his training and yours than by any other factor. Unless you seek a horse with a very high level of performance in a specialized activity, it is not difficult to find a horse who will serve you faithfully and well in a number of fields. And, if you give him the training, he might excel in one or more.

If you have young children and minimal space, a pony may be the right solution. Be sure a child knows the basics of good horsemanship before turning him loose with a pony.

A pony for the children?

Perhaps you are thinking of getting a pony for your small children. A child can participate in nearly as many horse activities with a pony as with a large horse and receive the same educational values.

A small pony is the least expensive way to start or participate in a horse hobby. Small ponies usually are inexpensive. At horse auctions large numbers of good ponies sell for $50 or less. In every community of horsepeople, there are plenty of families whose children have outgrown "Misty" and who will sell the pony for $50 if they are assured he will have a good home.

The facilities needed for a small pony are less than for a horse. Some kind of shelter is desirable, but not essential except in severe climates. Ponies' food requirements are lower in proportion to their smaller size. Fences to restrain them are less demanding than for a large horse. If you board the pony, the rate will be less than for a horse.

It is easier for a small child to handle and control a small animal. The hazards from falling off, having a foot stepped on, or being kicked should be less. But this comparison assumes a pony and a horse to be of equal training and equal disposition.

By making a minimal commitment in a small pony, you may be able to test the child's interest to determine whether this is a passing fancy or a more lasting interest before making greater investments.

However, a small child will quickly outgrow a small pony, and as a child's skills develop he may want greater challenges and opportunities than a small pony provides. Once Misty has become a member of the family you will find it very difficult to trade him in on a larger model, and you may end up with a pony and a horse, with need for only one.

The greater ease of handling and safety with a small pony may not materialize. Frequently small ponies are stubborn, balky, and perhaps kickers and biters. Perhaps this is the nature of the beast. But I suspect these are acquired rather than inherited traits, resulting from the pony's being handled mostly by children with little knowledge and skill in handling horses.

It is not difficult to obtain a *large* pony or small horse that is safe, meets the child's needs, and will serve his interests now and for years to come. My observations suggest that you consider this course of action. Before deciding what to buy, have your child take riding instructions. The odds are that the child will develop skill and confidence and you will be able to get a somewhat larger animal than you would otherwise. Usually this decision is more satisfactory in the long run.

Horse characteristics

Height

Many people think a horse must be tall for a tall man to ride, and very tall for a heavy person. Actually a horse's ability to carry weight is not determined by his height. Other features of his conformation, such as length of back, are more important. Some of the best "cow ponies," who carry cowboys for long distances over rugged terrain, are scarcely more than large ponies. Frequently 50- or 100-mile endurance rides are won by small horses carrying large men.

While individuals vary, large horses generally eat more because they have large bodies to maintain. They tear up the grass in the pasture more, and it takes a little stronger fence to restrain them. Frankly, I am biased in favor of a small and versatile horse for my use, between 14.3 and 15.2 hands. For the novice, a "hand" is 4 inches. The figure "14.3 hands" means 14 hands (56 inches) plus 3 inches, for a height of 59 inches, measured from the ground to the top of the withers.

Age

People frequently ask whether it is better to get a young horse or an old one. Considerations other than age probably are more important. Horses for general pleasure riding may be as young as three years or may be fully serviceable at twenty or older if kept in good health. Much depends on their past training, use, and treatment.

A horse has a long memory, especially for unpleasant or painful experiences, and you have no way of knowing what they have been. These experiences may lead to behavior that is undesirable. For example, your horse may act terrified at the sight of a whip, violently rebel when you try to apply a twitch, pull on the rope when you tie him, refuse to pass certain barriers on the trail, refuse to load into a trailer, or a multitude of other things. Or he may have had so much experience with beginners on his back that he recognizes them immediately and uses all the tricks he has learned for frustrating them.

On the other hand, the older horse probably has learned that he need not fear many of the things that to a young horse are new and terrifying. To the older horse, strange dogs suddenly appearing on the trail are no threat. He may even tolerate a motorcycle suddenly appearing from nowhere at full speed. He probably will recognize the beginning rider, but his response with a beginner aboard may be to go with special caution, and to do what he knows is right even when the signals from the rider seem to mean something else.

I had such a horse. Liza, with an experienced rider on board, was full of animation, high-stepping and always ready to go. But with a rider of little experience she walked slowly and carefully, never exceeded a slow trot, and ignored the enthusiasm of young riders for more speed.

In general, the old horse is more likely to have developed physical or psychological problems, but, if sound, he may have stood the test of time without bad habits.

A young horse is a clean slate. He lacks the learning that goes with experience and he may become frightened easily. His behavior in each new situation may be unpredictable. Your handling of him in new situations will be a major factor in determining his future disposition. If you are skillful, you may be able to mold a horse of superior temperament. If you are not skillful, you could ruin a young horse with great prospects.

Like people, younger horses will tend to have more energy, be more likely to fidget and fuss to get their own way, and take on each new experience with enthusiasm. This enthusiasm and energy, for the experienced rider, can add greatly to the joy of the sport.

Be sure to consider other factors along with age. A three-year-old with high intelligence, a calm disposition, and good training may be far more reliable than a fifteen-year-old of different disposition, training, and experience.

Mare or gelding?

You should consider the sex of the horse you get. You may consider a stallion, but unless yours is a very special situation, please take my advice and don't consider it for long if you are going to keep him on a small suburban or rural place. A horse's sex drive is very strong. With a stallion the fences have to be extra good, especially if neighbors have mares or if neighborhood children may ride mares past your place. A stallion may be just as gentle and easy to handle as an old mare for most of his life—but he can also be unpredictable, suddenly turning on his friends.

A mare has the advantage of providing the opportunity for breeding and all the enjoyment that goes with raising a foal. For a horse lover, there probably is no greater satisfaction than having your favorite mare bred; waiting anxiously for eleven months to see the results; watching the inquisitive, affectionate little devil run in the pasture; and raising the young one to become a fine horse. However, if you do this you will not get full recreational use of the mare for a time. Also, the reproductive cycle sometimes affects a mare's disposition. During the approximately five days out of twenty-one when a mare is in heat she may be more nervous, less easily controlled, or have other changes in disposition.

A gelding is a castrated male; he has lost his sex urge and lacks the behavioral traits related to sexuality. The gelding generally will have a more even disposition than either mare or stallion.

Consider bloodlines, conformation, temperament, and size when choosing a stallion to breed to your mare. This foal's dam is a Standardbred; the sire is a Trakehner.

Color

If you just *love* gray horses, you probably should have a gray horse. The color is only skin deep and does not affect his performance. However, in some breed organizations and related shows, color markings do make a difference. If you expect to participate in shows sponsored by a breed organization you should check the rules of the shows of that breed before buying.

Physical condition

There is an old saying, "No foot, no horse." You will want to be sure your horse is free of physical problems and defects that may interfere with your enjoyment of him.

A horse may have a multitude of physical problems or un-soundness: problems in vision, teeth, muscles, bones and joints, breathing, and hoofs. To be able to recognize all of them requires much experience and training—particularly if you are dealing with an old-fashioned horse trader.

You can buy a number of books that will help you know the complexity of the problem and alert you to some of the hazards. (I refer you to some in the Appendix.) It's a great disappoint-ment to fall in love with a horse, buy him, bring him home, and then discover he has a physical defect seriously limiting his use.

When you buy a horse, do not trust your limited knowledge of horse physiology and health. Even if you have had consid-erable experience with horses, you can be badly fooled. Take along a friend with more experience and then pay a veteri-narian to inspect the horse. This will cost you a few dollars but could save you hundreds of dollars and much regret and heart-ache.

Disposition

Horses' dispositions differ about as much as dispositions of people. If you are going to keep your horse in a confined situation in a community of many neighbors with curious and horse-loving children, the last thing you want is a mean or vicious animal. Also in such an area you won't want one who is easily alarmed by the sights and sounds of the suburbs.

You probably will want a horse who is quite tolerant of people, one who is a "people lover" yet accepts the authority and discipline of his master. You probably want a horse that enjoys his work—which means your pleasure. You will not want one who is inclined to bite or kick at people, or excessively at other horses, especially when you are riding in a group.

Performance

The final test is the answer to two questions: How does he perform for you? How does he behave? He may be beautiful, have innocent big brown eyes, carry his head like a champion, and fit your mental image of a perfect horse. But if he cannot do what you want him to, he is not the horse for you.

The only way you can find out how he performs is to ride him. If he is a good performer, the seller should not object to your giving him a good test. If you are indeed a greenhorn, totally lacking in training, trust a friend to test him for you. Also try to get some feeling for his disposition as you ride him and observe him around other horses.

In addition to physical defects that can limit the horse's performance, the horse may not walk, trot, canter, or perform other movements normally or the way you want him to. If you are not experienced in observing a horse's movements, you will need some advice. Watch him at various gaits and from different angles. A good judge of horses can tell much about his probable performance by studying his conformation. You, too, can learn to be a good observer and judge from books and friends. The Conformation Chart in this chapter will show you the parts of a horse to help you communicate with others about horses and their conformation.

Look at the horse as a whole, from some distance. If he seems symmetrical, balanced, athletic—if there is a unity to the animal, if the parts fit together smoothly—then chances are his conformation is pretty good.

Then develop the habit of seeing not the whole horse but specific parts, and compare the same parts on different horses to train yourself to see the details of the variation among animals. Until you do this it doesn't help you much if I say, "A horse should have a long neck."

A horse *should* have a long neck. He is almost certain to be a better performer if he does. His legs should be straight and squarely under him as seen from front, rear, and side. Obviously he shouldn't be "swaybacked"—have a big dip in his back. His shoulder bone should slope—the more the better—to give a spring to his ride. If that bone is vertical it will shake your bones every time he sets a foot down, especially when you are riding at the trot. The same goes for the pastern—the short bone just above the hoof—except it is a fault if this bone slopes too much.

What will a horse cost?

At this stage it may seem as though any horse that will pass the conformation and performance tests is bound to be very expensive. This is not necessarily so. You can buy a good horse who will perform very satisfactorily as a family pleasure horse for as little as $200 or $300 and as much more as you want to pay. As you pay more, you should be getting more for your money—in training, versatility, level of performance, potential as a breeding animal, beauty, disposition, or other ways. If you insist on a horse who is nearly perfect in all respects, you face a long search and will need to write a large check.

You may not think that it is possible to get a good horse for $200, but frequently people find it necessary to sell a family horse to which they have become attached, and to them the most important consideration in the sale may be a good home and devoted owners for this family member. If you want such a bargain take a little time and watch the newspaper ads. You might find that $200 will buy a horse that could cost you $1,000 from a dealer.

It takes time and money to train horses. The price of a very well-trained animal for any specialized activity will reflect these costs. A good, well-trained young hunter will probably be priced from $2,000 and up. The cost of a horse in a high state of training for cutting, barrel racing, or other specialties will be

Conformation Chart

Forehead
Poll
Muzzle
Underlip
Throat-latch
Neck
Crest
Withers
Back
Loin
Shoulder
Point of Shoulder
Chest
Arm
Elbow
Forearm
Knee
Barrel
Rump
Point of hip
Buttock
Thigh
Flank
Stifle
Abdomen
Girth
Gaskin
Hock
Fetlock
Coronet
Cannon
Ankle
Pastern
Hoof

in the same price range. With old age or impaired health, of course, the price will decline considerably.

If you buy from a breeding farm or a dealer don't expect to buy a very good horse for $200. The operator of the farm is trying to make money raising horses—and that is difficult. At least he wants to get back the money it has cost him to breed, keep, and train the horse. Think of his expenses: it probably cost him at least $300 to feed and care for the broodmare during the year she was in foal (and she will not foal every year). If she is a $3,000 mare he will have costs of depreciation and interest on her of perhaps $600 per year. The cost of breeding the mare was from $100 up. Then he had to feed and care for the offspring for three years and train it before it was ready for you to buy and ride. During all this time he paid for feed, veterinarian bills, taxes, labor, and so on. If he sells a horse for less than $1,000 he surely is losing money.

If you buy a horse from anyone for less than $1,000, someone along the way has sold it for less than his costs. Perhaps that person figured that he got his money back through the use he made of the animal. If you sell yours, you may have to figure that way too. Statistics are not available on horse sales, but it appears that most horses sold for pleasure use have sold for less than $1,000.

Like most of us, you may find it necessary to compromise your desire for perfection with your ability to pay. If so, do not compromise on health and soundness. Remember—no foot, no horse. Do not compromise much on disposition, either, at least not to the extent of buying a horse who may not be safe to have in your backyard.

Frequently people reason that since they want only enjoyment from simple trail-riding, they might as well buy an inexpensive horse. They may get one lacking in performance abilities, beauty, or disposition. As their skills develop with experience and their interests expand, they find that this horse is not what they want. This method of getting started can be very satisfactory. My family went through this process, but we had a difficult time overcoming our reluctance to change horses.

Other prospective buyers reason that, since it costs no more to keep a good horse, they may as well start out with a more expensive horse. Also, they reason, you should be able to sell the horse and get your money back. If you elect this course, be sure to remember that your horse can die or develop physical problems that may cause his value to drop considerably. And, like you and me, he is sure to age. You can buy insurance to reduce the risk of loss from death, but this adds another expense. Also, if you have a very valuable horse you may want more expensive fences and better housing to help protect your investment.

The old-fashioned art of horse trading

Simply stated, a horse is worth whatever the seller can persuade the buyer to pay.

Horses vary so much in their characteristics that it's very difficult to say a horse of such-and-such quality is worth so many dollars. Buying and selling horses is much different from dealing in products that are highly standardized or are traded in large volume. There is no "blue book" to go by as there is in the used-car business.

Much dickering is frequently involved in arriving at a sale price for a horse. Sometimes the asking price may be adjusted upward according to the seller's estimate of the prospective buyer's ability to pay. For example, if you go into a horse dealer's place and let him know you want a $1,000 horse, you may find that all of his horses suddenly went up in value to at least that amount.

Early in the history of this country, and probably before that, horse traders developed a reputation that often was justly deserved. Horse trading exemplified the principle of "caveat emptor"—"let the buyer beware." In trading horses it was considered acceptable for the trader to do almost anything to avoid revealing the inadequacies of a horse and to lead the buyer to believe the animal had good qualities. Horse dealers became very skilled at making a lame horse appear sound, a blind horse appear to be able to see, a lazy horse seem full of pep, and a mean horse seem gentle.

Horse trading has not changed very much since those days—except that modern science has provided new techniques for a horse trader of dubious ethics to use.

Many sellers of horses are completely reliable and would never consider misleading the buyer. But others emulate the traditional horse trader of grandfather's day.

Where to buy a horse

If you look around your area and study the ads in the local paper, you will find livestock auctions with horse sales at weekly or monthly intervals within an easy drive. These auctions generally sell any horse brought to the sale, regardless of its condition.

You may want to go to such a sale for an educational and entertaining evening, but exercise great discipline (or sit on your hands) when an apparent beauty comes in the ring and seems to be selling below his value. Unless you really know horses, at such an auction you have no way of knowing how skillful a horse trader the seller is.

To hear it, every horse coming into the ring has good qualities. "This horse is a real baby-sitter, safe for any child to ride," may mean that the horse is old, sick, lazy, and almost totally lacking in desire to work. Tranquilizers and pain-killing drugs may be used on some of the horses, but you have no way of knowing this until you get the horse home. You may notice that a very high proportion of the horses being sold are nine years old and conclude that there must have been a big crop of foals nine years ago. Not so. The real reason is that a horse's teeth tell a horse's age quite well up to nine years, but after that provide only a basis for a guess.

Also within an easy drive of your place there probably are several horse dealers with a number of horses on hand for you to look over. Many such dealers take pride in selling good horses and carefully guard a reputation for fair and honest deals. Others operate more like the horse traders of old. If you talk with some of the horsemen in your community, you should be able to obtain information that will help you select a horse dealer to suit you. Your veterinarian will be an excellent source of information.

Inside the barn at the weekly horse auction in Plain, Wisconsin. Horses from as far away as Wyoming are brought to be sold, and "caveat emptor" is the rule of the day.

Purebred auctions provide another alternative for buying your horse. You probably have heard of the annual sales at Saratoga Springs, New York, or at the Keeneland track in Lexington, Kentucky. These are specialized sales where young horses bred for racing are sold, some for very fancy prices indeed. There are many less well known sales where only purebred stock of a certain breed is sold. Some organizations hold purebred consignment sales at which breeders sell their horses. For example, almost any week of the year there is a purebred Arabian auction somewhere in the country, and there is bound to be at least one Arabian sale a year within driving distance of your home. These sales are usually advertised in one or more of the breed magazines. (A list of magazines is provided in the Appendix.)

You are likely to read about the highest price paid at one of these sales, or the average price of the top horses, and think it is no place for you to buy. Although the primary function of these sales is a service to breeders who are interested in buying or selling breeding stock, often among the horses sold are those the breeder has used for pleasure riding or farm work, show horses, mares that have encountered breeding difficulties, young stallions with limited prospects as breeders, or geldings that have not been sold through other channels. Many of these horses make the finest family pleasure and show horses. (Of course, if you bought a stallion at such a sale you would want to have him gelded.) At such a sale you might well buy a very fine animal with extensive training for no more money than you would pay for a grade horse of uncertain value.

Typically, the operators of these auctions have a veterinarian at the sale to examine each animal and present the results of his examination to all prospective buyers. Also, plenty of time is generally provided before the sale for you to inspect and ride any horse you are interested in. Some sales may guarantee that all horses are sound except for any problems pointed out by the veterinarian and the auction management.

You may also buy directly from a horse breeder at his farm. Breeders of purebreds generally are very interested in satisfied customers and word-of-mouth advertising. Some will provide you with training to be sure you and the horse are "on the same wave length," and many will sell on an installment plan.

The want ads in your local paper and in the many horse magazines may also be a good way to locate a horse, as long as you have an opportunity to observe the kind of treatment the animal has had. Take the time to inspect the horse, ride it, and have it checked by an expert. You may find a very good buy from someone who is in a hurry to sell, or someone who wants the horse. to have a good home and places this above price.

You may also buy a horse from a trainer or owner at a race track. Frequently when these people are in need of money they will sell for a few hundred dollars a horse who does not show high prospects for winning. Such a horse may become a fine family pleasure horse, hunter, jumper, or show animal. But bear in mind that the animal's training probably has been directed at one thing—winning races—and he may not have the disposition and training you want. For example, he may know only one way to go with a person on his back—full speed ahead. After a period of rest you may be able to retrain him quite successfully. You should keep in mind that racing is hard on the feet and legs; many race horses develop foot and leg problems that can seriously limit their ability to perform for you. If you consider buying such a horse, you would be smart to have him inspected by a vet before you close the deal.

4

Horse sense: knowing and handling your horse

Horses, like people, have personalities. I have two horses who are half-brother and half-sister but who are quite different. Suie is affectionate—I stand in the pasture and she rubs her head on my arm, nibbles at my shirt, or nudges me with her nose. She is cautious, and when something strange appears she hangs back while other horses investigate the dangers. She also is patient and will stand for an hour while I groom and polish her even though she wants to be in the pasture with the others. Her gelded brother Count, in contrast, is the courageous one, always first to challenge some new cause for alarm. He is impatient and never wants to stand around for a lot of foolishness.

Affectionate, cautious, patient, courageous: all are terms we use to describe human personalities as well as horses. In fact, someone observed that a horse tends to have the disposition of his owner. This is likely to be the case if he has had the horse for

50

a while and if he and the horse have spent much time together, because of the many interactions between man and horse.

For pleasure and safety, you as a horse owner need to know your horse and to communicate with him. The better you understand his mental processes, the better you can understand and control his actions. When you understand his motivations and the stimuli to which he responds, you can use them to obtain from him the behavior you desire. For safety, you need to know his fears and his reactions to various situations.

Each horse is unique, just as each person is. He has his own personality, the product of his inheritance, his environment, and his experience. Probably there is as much variety among horses in this regard as among people. You need to know your horse, his individuality, his idiosyncrasies.

My objective here is to provide the new horse owner enough knowledge of horse psychology and behavior, in general, to help him get started on the process of knowing and handling his horse.

The horse's senses

Smell and hearing

Healthy horses have very acute hearing and sense of smell, much more acute than yours or mine. Your horse probably will love to eat apples and carrots. To me a carrot doesn't have much odor, but when I go to the barn with a carrot in my jacket the horse knows it is there instantly. He will check out that pocket each time he sees me for several days—either because the odor lingers or because he remembers the treat. If you eat an apple and go to see your horse an hour later without washing your hands, he will smell the apple and expect a handout.

I had one horse who had to receive much painful treatment from a veterinarian. After a few visits she began to get upset when the vet entered the barn. For years she "turned tail" whenever any veterinarian came into the pasture where she was grazing. My only explanation was that she could detect the odor of medicines and disinfectants, which reminded her of her pain.

Frequently you will notice when riding on trails that your horse knows about the approach of another rider long before you do. Or you may observe that when a horse and rider are returning from a ride, even when they are still over the horizon the horses left at home know about their return. This communication is by hearing and smell and perhaps through vibrations transmitted through the ground.

You will notice that your horse flicks his ears often, sometimes pricking them forward, sometimes turning them toward the side. He does this to complement his eyesight in determining the position and sources of sounds. Blind horses move their ears incessantly, using them as receivers to plot the direction and distance of objects by the sounds they make.

Sight

The horse sees differently than people do, for the horse's eye has a different physical structure than the human eye. In both animals light passes through the lens to hit the retina at an angle, but the horse's retina (unlike that of a human) is *irregularly* concave. Therefore, the horse must raise or lower his head to let light rays strike at the angle that will produce the clearest image—one angle for distance, another for close-ups. A horse will raise his head to focus on close objects and lower it to see distant objects. (In both cases he will have a "blind spot" either above or below the area he's focusing on.)

In addition, the horse, like many other animals, is color-blind; he sees mostly masses of various shades and shapes of gray, with little detail. Anything that moves is singled out by the horse for attention—either as something to be investigated or something from which to flee.

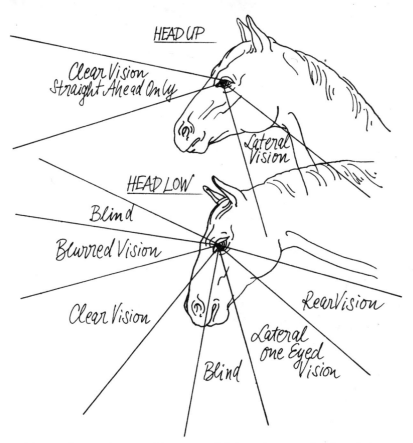

HEAD UP

Clear Vision Straight Ahead Only

Lateral Vision

HEAD LOW

Blind

Blurred Vision

Clear Vision

Rear Vision

Lateral one Eyed Vision

Blind

Although horses have a wide range of vision, they see clearly only in a limited area. Even a familiar object can seem threatening or distorted if it is glimpsed laterally or outside the zone of good binocular vision.

The horse's vision is complicated by the fact that, due to the widespread placement of his eyes, he also has lateral vision, and, to a degree, posterior vision. A horse sees two images at once—one on either side—when his eyes are not focused ahead. He cannot get a true understanding of the depth of the side object unless he turns his head to focus both eyes on it. The reason race horses often wear blinkers is to reduce the distractions of lateral vision and force the horse to focus straight ahead, on the finish line.

These characteristics of horse vision have practical application for the rider. So that a horse can use his forward binocular vision to best advantage, the rider should let his horse move his head freely to focus on near and distant objects as he needs to. If something approaches a horse from the rear, where he cannot see well, he may react with a quick kick before turning his head to look. This leads to an important safety rule: Don't approach a horse from the rear, or if you do, speak to him as you go. Occasionally an object that is glimpsed on only one side—such as a piece of paper flying in the wind—may frighten a horse if he is not allowed to get a good look at it.

The two-sided nature of his vision and other features of his nervous system sometimes result in the horse's reacting differently to an object when it is on one side of him than the other. When he is being exposed to objects new to him, it may be necessary for him to get acquainted with them on both sides. Also, a strange object may look entirely different to him from one side compared to the other. On the trail, if you come to something that frightens him and then get him to accept it, you may need to work out the problem again when you come from the other direction.

Voice and touch: communication

Over the centuries that man has lived with horses he has developed methods of communicating his desires to them, based on some of the horse's characteristics. These communication devices must be learned anew by each generation of horses—and horsemen.

Horses communicate with one another but they have a real problem teaching humans to communicate with them. Smart horses are good students of human behavior and quickly learn to understand man.

The most obvious method of communication among horses is by voice. Different cries clearly communicate different meanings to other horses. With a little practice you will be able to listen in on this communication.

One cry clearly says, "Come home, I am lonely." Another

says, "Where are you?" Others say, "I am in pain," or "I'm glad to see you." Once you learn this language, you will find that they use it in talking to you, just as you use English on them.

They have other methods of communication. Just as you and I communicate messages to one another by the way we hold our heads and hands, by our facial expressions, and by the tone of our voices, so do horses communicate in a variety of ways.

One way of swishing the tail may say, "Get away from me." If one horse sees something to be afraid of and suddenly jumps into a gallop, the others receive the message before that horse makes his first stride. One way of stamping the foot may be just an effort to move the flies, while another stamp says, "I don't like that—quit it."

By carefully observing your horse you will learn a lot about what he is thinking, in addition to receiving messages he

A rider communicates with her horse by voice, through subtle tension on the reins, and by pressure from legs and heels.

intentionally sends you. You will know when he is paying attention to you or is distracted, when he is cautiously studying something, when he is alert or frightened, and when he is about to turn, kick, run, or execute some other maneuver. This knowledge will enable you to take action appropriate to the situation.

Similarly, the horse will be reading you. Very quickly he will learn when you are coming to dish out feed. A bang of the stable door or a rattle of the feed can will tell him that chow is ready, and he will come bounding from the far corner of the pasture.

If you are frightened while riding, he will know it instantly from the tension of your body and the tone of your voice. He also "reads" special movements you make—the pressure of your leg, a jerk of your hand, a shift of your weight. He is likely to assume that when you are frightened he should be frightened too, and may break into a run if you are riding. Do your best to remain calm, no matter what happens. In situations that are hazardous, make a special effort to communicate confidence to your horse. He will sense your confidence, just as he can sense your fear. The chances are high that if you are relaxed and happy your horse will be too.

A suburban horseman may have one advantage over those in a more rural setting. While in the pasture, his horse will become accustomed to rushing fire engines, wailing sirens, roaring motorcycles, large trucks, strange dogs, newspapers blowing in the pasture, and a variety of other things that sometimes terrorize a horse on the trail. But this horse may be struck with terror when he first encounters a cow.

Older horses can detect the difference between an experienced horseman and a "greenhorn" the minute a person comes in the barn. Some horses, with a beginner on board, will be very careful, walking slowly as befits the skill of the rider. Other horses in such circumstances disregard all signals the rider gives, or even try to test the rider to see how green he really is. Such a horse was one I remember from my college days. All freshmen in the College of Agriculture had to take a test to determine their mastery of farm skills. One skill tested was that of harnessing a horse, for which an old draft horse was regularly used. A farm boy who had done the job before could harness the horse easily while the horse stood motionless. When a city boy tried, even if thoroughly instructed in advance by his country friends, the horse would shake his head and step away at just the right time to keep the city boy from getting one piece of harness in place.

When working around your horse, it is a good idea to talk to him. It doesn't matter much what you say, but be sure to talk in a calm, confident tone. You can train your horse to execute certain movements when you say certain words, but the horse receives messages from you more by the tone of your voice than from the words you use.

The back and sides of a horse are very sensitive. As you sit on his back he feels your every movement. Perhaps through the actions of your muscles he knows when you want to speed up, slow down, or stop. At any rate, when you have spent a lot of time in the saddle, the way you sit or move a leg or hand will mean something definite to your horse, and he will seem to respond instinctively to your desires, almost as though the two bodies were controlled by one mind.

Moods and emotions

Like people, horses have their moods. You sometimes wake up on the "wrong" side of the bed. Some days you may have a backache, sore feet, or a headache. On such days you may be a little hard to live with. Your horse has the same problems, only he cannot tell you about his moods in the language to which you are accustomed. But once you have developed the ability to recognize and understand his signals—the position of his ears, the way he holds his neck, eyes, and nostrils, the way he

A horse "laughing"—but most horsemen agree he actually is smelling something new.

swishes his tail—you will be able to tell something about his mood. The way he acts around other horses and the way he responds to a pat on the neck or to a brushing also reveal how he feels.

When you let your horse out of the stall and he goes running and bucking through the pasture, head held high, ears pointed up, eyes large and flashing, nostrils flared, you know he is feeling well. But if he mopes by himself in one corner of the pasture, head drooping, eyes half shut, ears laid back, paying little attention to you or the other horses, chances are he is not feeling so well.

Mares frequently have moody spells related to the estrous cycle. If you go to saddle your mare and she protests a little, objects to being brushed, or shies at common objects along the trail, she may be in heat. Stallions also seem to have one-track minds at times. Geldings, lacking the reproductive processes and sex drives of either sex, are less moody and more even or reliable in temperament.

A horse has about the same emotions as you and I—fear, curiosity, love, hate, anger, and so on. The horse's normal response to fear is to turn and run. If he is not badly frightened or only cautious, he may stand with muscles tense and ready for flight, head held high, ears, eyes, and nostrils straining to learn more about the source of the fright.

The horse is inevitably curious, as well as alert to possible danger, when something new appears in his environment. First he may circle the strange object, prepared for instant flight. When it does not bite, he will use all his senses to learn more about the object—sniff it, touch with his nose, paw at it, perhaps bite it—and then ignore it.

Horses develop strong affections for one another and for people. Two horses may be inseparable, scratching each other's back and pining when separated. When his person comes around, the horse may rub his head on him or her, follow him or her through the pasture, and perhaps run and kick with glee. Similarly a horse may develop hate for an individual who has mistreated him, and will obviously display this emotion. When a horse is really angry at another horse he may lay his ears back along his neck, bare his teeth, and perhaps charge.

The horse, like other animals, feels heat, cold, pain, and irritation. He responds by trying to relieve the discomfort by whatever methods experience has told him are likely to work. This characteristic of the horse is used by man in training and in developing communications. For example, a horse's sides are sensitive, and if there is pressure on his ribs on one side, he moves away from the pressure. This relieves the discomfort and becomes a part of his behavior pattern. It also provides a way for a rider to tell him to move to the right or left.

Motivation

Psychologists studying people have found that we seek recognition, satisfaction from accomplishment, and approval. Most of us respond to the opportunity to satisfy these needs. We are likely to work much harder, with much more enthusiasm and dedication in our jobs, if we experience these satisfactions as we go along.

We may also work because of punishment or the threat of punishment. But generally, a person who does certain things in his job under a threat of being fired is not enthusiastic or creative in his work.

While psychologists have not studied the horse as thoroughly as they've studied man, these principles seem to apply to horses too. The experiences of most horse trainers seem to confirm this conclusion. Successful trainers rely much more on positive reinforcements—rewards and praise—than

A chunk of carrot rewards the horse for good behavior—and encourages him to repeat it.

on the threat of punishment. For horses, the carrot is literally better than the stick.

When a horse does what you want or does something particularly well, you may give him a pat on the neck or a chunk of carrot. It may be just as effective to give him a few words of praise. After such rewards he seems to hold his head a little higher and go about his work with more pride and enthusiasm, and he will try to figure out what he did that resulted in this reward, and do it again.

At a horse show, some horses going forward to receive an award seem to sense that they are being recognized and leave the ring with an air of pride. Your pride as the rider is almost certain to be telegraphed to the horse.

When horses were in common use as beasts of burden, there were many situations where moving a load required an extra effort from a team of horses pulling in absolute unison. Some teamsters approached such a situation with a whip, much yelling, and no small amount of profanity. Other teamsters said a few words of encouragement, walked alongside the team, and lavishly expressed their praise and thanks when the job was done. The latter type of teamster seemed to get more from his horses and with less effort.

There is probably nothing more important for the horseman to remember than to praise and thank his horse for doing right (not just for exceptional performance) and to use punishment and rebuke most sparingly. Once this practice becomes a habit he may also find himself applying it more fully to people in his family, his place of work, and his community. If so, the results may justify all the costs of a horse hobby!

Using psychology in training

We mentioned that a horse acts to relieve discomforts or irritations, for example, by moving away from pressure. If a rider leans forward, this places extra weight on the horse's front legs, so he moves forward to achieve greater balance.

Once the movement the horse makes achieves the results he desires, he remembers this and acts similarly the next time. Rewarding this action with praise (or a carrot) generally strengthens his response the next time. With repetition, the response to a mild application of the stimulus becomes almost automatic. He learns that this is your signal for telling him what you want him to do.

Training a horse to perform tricks relies on this principle. For example, when a fly bites the horse on the neck he learns at an early age to shake his head to relieve the discomfort. This fact is used to teach a horse to say "No." Prick him on the neck in the right spot and he will shake his head as though to get rid of a fly. Reward him. With frequent repetition he learns to say "No" to your questions with just a light touch on that spot in the neck.

The horse can learn bad habits or undesirable responses through this process as well. If he acts up when you are riding him because of his displeasure with the weight on his back or out of rebellion to discipline, and you "reward" him by turning him out to pasture, he has learned a lesson. He can be depended on to act up again when he wants his freedom.

From this follows a good rule: Always quit when you are ahead. If you have a problem, quit riding before the horse starts acting up or stay with him until he does right, and then turn him out.

Another case along the same line may be the horse who rushes toward home when he's on the trail. This horse may have found that by hurrying home he quickly gets rid of his burden or receives the reward he seeks—being turned out to pasture. If you have this problem, don't give him that reward as soon as you get home. Instead, ride him hard for a while, and give him some rest and reward while you're still out on the trail.

As you work with your horse, be careful that you are not rewarding behavior that is undesirable.

Punishment

Punishing a horse is a special case of the reinforcement principle. If he does something undesirable and you immediately do something unpleasant to him, he will associate the cause and the effect. With repetition, he will learn to avoid the act that brings an uncomfortable consequence. But he will not know what caused the punishment unless it follows immediately after the act. Therefore, a rule to be strictly followed is that punishment must be administered immediately.

Use no more punishment than necessary. A sharp, authoritative "Stop it!" may be enough. A light, quick strike on the rump with the crop, if you are riding, may convey the message. A sharp jerk on the lead rope will be an unpleasant reminder. But *never* strike a horse about the head and do not hit to hurt. It is enough to do something that is unpleasant, not painful. If you lose your temper, you may hurt the horse physically and also cause a new set of horse behavior problems worse than the ones you are trying to cure.

Never punish a horse for being afraid. If he is frightened by something and you punish him for his reaction, you have succeeded only in confirming his fears. He saw the object that he thought would hurt him, and he did feel pain. There is a better way to handle such a situation. For example, if you are riding on the trail and your horse is frightened by some strange object, do not use the crop. Instead talk to him and let him know that you are not afraid. Give him confidence that he will not be hurt, quietly urge him on, and then praise him.

Memory

Horses have long memories for situations that have resulted in pain or severe discomfort, but also for situations that are rewarding to them.

If you are out for a ride and let your horse eat for a while in a nice patch of grass, he probably will try to stop there the next time you pass. If something frightens him at some spot on the trail, he'll be very alert when you pass there again.

Several years ago I rode a newly acquired horse on an unfamiliar trail. In a straight level area there was mud in which the horse slipped and nearly fell. I did not travel that trail again for a year. The second time it was dry and dusty. At precisely the spot where she had slipped a year before, the horse slowed down and walked carefully around the spot that had been a pool of mud. Horses have excellent memories for terrain. After you have been over a trail once, your horse probably will know the way home.

Horse social order

In a group of horses there always is a so-called "pecking order." Each horse has its position in the social hierarchy. The horse at the top has special privileges and rights. For example, throw a pile of hay in the pasture and the Number One horse will eat first, even if you think another needs it more. Open a gate for horses to go out to fresh pasture and Number One probably will go first. If it is raining and the shelter is crowded, the horses near the top of the order will get preference over others for staying dry.

This is the way it is in the horse society and you are not going to change it, even if you think your favorite little mare should have preference over that old gelding.

A horse likes company. In the herd, each horse seems to derive a feeling of security from his place in the pecking order, low though it may be. If he doesn't have another horse for company he may enjoy the company of a dog, goat, cat, pony, or other animal. Sometimes such animals become inseparable pals and the horse pines when his pal is away.

Introduce a new horse into a herd and his place in the social order must be established. The ritual for this includes much running and bucking. You can shorten the process some and reduce the violence by letting them get acquainted over a fence or a stall door, but they must go through their ritual. You won't have much to say about where the new horse fits in. Don't tie a horse in a paddock with other horses running loose: a horse lower in the order than the tied horse may see this as a fine opportunity to challenge his position, and the tied horse may be injured as a result.

There is a constant process of order maintenance, as some "social climbers" seek to rise higher in the order and the challenged seek to maintain their positions. If your horses bare their teeth or kick at one another occasionally, this is just a part of their social competition.

If you feed hay or grain in the paddock, recognize the pecking order and have the feed so distributed, or your facilities so arranged, that the horses on the bottom of the order can get their share—not just what is left when the others have had their fill.

Loading a horse into a trailer

The principle of the learned response is the basis of much useful training, including teaching your horse to walk into a trailer. There are a number of techniques used successfully. Your animal may be so well trained and have so much confidence in you that you can lead him in the first time you try—but probably not. First he must overcome his fear of that strange, confining place. A good way to accomplish this is to leave the trailer in the pasture with the door open so he can investigate it as his curiosity prompts him. Then feed his grain in it. After a few days of this he will walk in readily when you feed—and this is one way to load a horse. Tie the halter rope while he is eating, close the door, and you are ready to go. After this, just entice him with a little grain each time you want to load him.

Another approach is to make him a little uncomfortable until

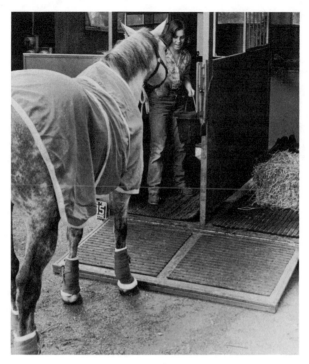

Many horses can be lured into a trailer with a bucket of grain. If you haul your horse often, it is wise to use protective leg wraps, tail bandages, and a head guard. In cold weather, a light blanket may be in order.

he starts in, and then remove the source of discomfort. Some trainers use a crop held over the horse's back and lightly flicked across the base of the tail to create the discomfort. Others tie a rope to the trailer, bring it around behind the horse as he faces the trailer door, and lightly drape it across the back of his legs. He doesn't like that and goes in to avoid it. But you will never get him in by beating and whipping him—nor can you pull or push him in unless he has decided to quit the foolishness and go in. Sometimes it helps to load another first, preferably one of your horse's companions. This may tell him there is nothing to fear. Sometimes nothing seems to work very well and great patience may be required.

How to catch a horse

Most families have experienced periods of several days of bad weather when the small children were kept in the house. As time drags on, the children get nervous, fuss and fidget, and tempers flare. When the sun shines and they finally go out to play, they seem to go wild for a while.

A horse confined to a small stall will act much like a child on a rainy day. When he first is free he is full of energy and may submit to your will reluctantly. You will be wise to let him use up some of that energy before you ride, particularly if he is a young horse and you are not an accomplished rider. You can do this by exercising him a few minutes on a longe line.

When your horse breaks out of the pasture he may have a similar reaction. You will soon learn how to catch horses, but a word of advice may save you some trouble.

There seems to be nothing a horse enjoys more than a race across suburban lawns with a flock of yelling children and barking dogs in hot pursuit. Chasing a horse is not the way to catch him.

Before the children and dogs take up the chase, quietly get a pail of grain and a halter. Slowly approach the horse, perhaps acting reluctant for him to have any of the grain. His curiosity will be aroused by the pail and once he smells the grain he will forget all the other attractions, and you'll have him.

What if he's broken out and you don't see him anywhere? He will probably respond to one of three impulses—to enjoy his freedom by racing and bucking across the countryside, to eat some of that fresh unspoiled grass on the other side of the fence, or to seek the company of other horses. If he responds to the first, his attention will soon switch to the second or third. So look for him grazing in an extra-green and succulent patch of grass or standing along someone's fence talking to other horses—or perhaps waiting in a barn where a helpful neighbor put him after finding the horse in his garden corn patch. In

If your horse gets loose—or even if he's hard to catch in your own pasture—a bait of grain will usually bring him within reach.

fact, horses love corn, and if there is a cornfield near by, that is where he will be.

While I'm on the subject of horses that are loose I want to raise the question of your liability. You probably are legally responsible for any damage the horse does. You may also be liable for damages to a car and its occupants if a car hits your horse. You better consult your insurance agent on these points and discuss the adequacy of your insurance.

Like people, horses never stop learning. Each new experience provides a new cause–effect relationship and remains in the horse's memory. The new experience may confirm and reinforce old experience. Or a new experience may lead the horse to some new path of behavior, which from the human point of view could be better or worse.

You cannot force a horse to do as you wish. In any test of physical strength a man is sure to lose. The horse will do as you wish only because he wants to—because he understands you and wants to please you, because he trusts you, because he thinks the action will be satisfying to him, or because it seems to be the way to avoid displeasure.

As long as you have and use a horse, you will be challenged to know him and his mind. If you succeed at that, you will be able to do the things that make him a model horse.

♞ 5
Horse care

"For the want of a nail a shoe was lost. For the want of a shoe a horse was lost. . . ." This old refrain emphasizes the need for attention to management—and attention to the little details that are important.

To fully enjoy horse-keeping, you should take care of your horse and keep him healthy. You will enjoy the horse most if he is feeling well. You will want to take care of your land and fences so you can be proud of them, too. And you will want to do these things without spending so much of your time on management that you have none left for riding. Also, you must consider costs.

Horse nutrition

Good health starts with good nutrition, with horses just as with people. There is much that is not known about the nutrition and feeding of horses, especially the quality of nutrition needed to obtain high levels of performance and long productive lives. There has been a great volume of research on the nutrition and feeding of poultry, hogs, beef cattle, and dairy cattle, but comparatively little on horses. With the other animals, the objectives are to obtain high quality eggs, milk, or

Good pasture and clean water provide a complete horse diet.

meat at low cost. Length of productive life and athletic ability are not the high priority considerations that they are with the horse, so relating the results of research on those animals to horses is of limited value.

But a certain amount of fact about the nutrition and feeding of horses has been established. I will not go into detail here, but refer you to the bibliography in the Appendix. My emphasis will be on practical application.

All animals, including man, have some common nutritional needs. All need carbohydrates to provide energy, protein (including essential amino acids) for growth and body maintenance, and salt, iron, and a long list of other minerals in small amounts. All need the same vitamins, although in different quantities and proportions. All need a certain amount of fiber to provide bulk in the diet. All need water. All of these nutritional elements have to be available in the right quantities and combinations to produce a healthy animal.

The digestive system of the horse is especially equipped for his diet. He has a large intestine with great capacity for holding the vegetation or hay he eats. Large numbers of bacteria attack the plant fibers and begin a series of chemical reactions that causes the proteins, vitamins, and carbohydrates to be released and absorbed by the body. If a horse goes a long time between feedings, the bacteria finish their work and perish, and are not present in sufficient numbers when a new supply of feed is consumed.

Horses are like people in that there are many differences among them in how they burn calories. One horse will get fat on a ration that will keep another slim and sleek. One will be skin and bones on a ration that keeps another in good shape. Horses who require little feed to stay in shape are called "easy keepers."

A young growing animal has different nutritional requirements than an old animal. The young one needs more protein, minerals, and vitamins to build bone and muscle as he grows, while the old horse needs only to maintain his body and energy.

A pregnant mare has no special nutritional requirements until about the last three months of pregnancy. At that time the foal grows rapidly and the mother must have extra quantities of grain to provide the energy, protein, and vitamins needed for the growth of the young. After the birth, cut down on feed for a day or two, and then feed her extra rations to produce the increasing quantities of milk the foal will need.

Nutritional needs also depend on the activity of the animal. Work requires energy, which must come from the energy stored in the body as fat. The active animal must have adequate nutrition to maintain and repair the body parts that are affected by greater use.

The amount of hay or feed an animal needs also depends on the quality of the feed—that is, the amount of all the essential nutrients it contains. The extent to which the horse is infested with parasites is another consideration.

With all these variables no one can tell you just how much hay and grain you will need to feed your horse. But by observing him you can tell pretty well how healthy he is. A well nourished horse generally is in good flesh. He looks "thrifty." He has a sleek, shiny coat. His eyes sparkle. He looks alert and full of pep.

Even though I cannot tell you how much feed your horse will need the following chart will provide a good guide.

HORSE FEEDING GUIDE
(Adapted from *Breeding and Raising Horses*, USDA Handbook No. 394)

1. *Mature idle horses weighing 900 to 1400 lbs.*
   Daily allowance:
   1-1/2 to 1-3/4 lb. of grass or mixed hay per 100 lb. of body weight. With grass hay, feed additional 3/4 lb. of high-protein supplement daily.
2. *Mature horses at work (riding, driving, racing) weighing 900 to 1400 lbs.*
   Daily allowance:
   Light work—2/5 to 1/2 lb. of grain and 1-1/4 to 1-1/2 lb. of grass hay per 100 lb. of body weight.
   Medium work—3/4 to 1 lb. of grain and 1 to 1-1/4 lb. of grass hay per 100 lb. of body weight.
   Hard work—1-1/4 to 1-1/2 lb. of grain and 1 to 1-1/4 lb. of grass hay per 100 lb. of body weight.

"Grain" refers to a good commercial mix of horse feed. Also provide free access to salt.

Pasture grasses are the natural feed of horses. Good pasture will provide all the protein, vitamins, and minerals the horse needs for good health. If you have a good pasture, most horses will not need grain unless they are doing hard work. The horses of most recreation owners seldom work very hard. On the other hand, few of them have good pasture.

How much pasture do you need for each horse? It depends on how well grass grows in your climate and on your soil, how many weeds there are, how well it is fertilized, and other factors. But as a rough guide for good soil in parts of the country receiving adequate spring and summer rain, you'll need two acres per horse. You might get by with one acre if you manage the pasture very well.

Hay

Hay is the standard feed for horses. It is the least expensive form of roughage grass. You will need hay at least during the winter months, unless you provide a complete pelleted feed. Feeding some hay even in summer will help conserve your limited supply of pasture and make it produce better. In most areas, it costs less to feed hay than pellets, but you should compare costs. If you cannot get good hay, you may prefer pellets, which are scientifically prepared to serve the nutritional needs of horses.

Good hay, like good pasture, is all the feed most mature horses need to keep them in good shape unless they are doing hard work or are in foal. A young horse, still growing rapidly, should have some supplemental grain even with good hay.

It is not always easy to obtain good hay. Some that is on sale for horsemen provides very little nutrition, and is a waste of money. To buy good hay you need to be able to identify it. Standardized hay grades are not in general use by many growers who sell hay for horses, but with just a little experience, you can become a fairly good judge of hay.

The hay on the inside of a bale should be a bright green color—the greener the better. Green hay is high in protein and vitamins. The outer surface may be bleached by the sun, but it is the color on the inside of the bale that counts. It should consist of grasses or a mixture of grasses and clover or alfalfa. You can feed straight clover or alfalfa hay but this sometimes causes digestive problems. Stick with a hay that is mostly grass and you can give the horse all he can eat without causing any problems. The hay should not have a moldy or musty odor or appearance. It should contain a lot of the leaves of the grass and legumes, not just a lot of stems. There should be few weeds or briars. Many of the weed seeds in the hay will end up in your pasture to grow next summer and plague you again and again.

Much of the hay offered to horsemen is harvested from nearby land by an energetic person with an eye on opportunities to make a few dollars. Such a field is likely to contain many weeds, and the grasses may not be the best for horse nutrition. Frequently, such hay is cut when it is overripe and has lost much of its feed value. You can feed this hay successfully if it is not moldy, but it will be very limited in nutritional values. You will need to supplement it with grain and probably some minerals and vitamins. If good hay is very expensive, this may be your most satisfactory answer.

Your local feedstore may sell low quality hay, or it may offer hay produced by a farmer who makes a business of selling high-quality hay. If the feedstores do not have high-quality hay, you may be able to find a farmer or rancher who will provide the kind you want and deliver it to your stable.

The quantity to be fed depends on your horse, how much exercise he gets, and the quality of your feed. Numerous books and magazine articles provide information to guide you. However, the final test is the condition of your horse. If he is getting too fat on what you are feeding him, cut back on the grain. If he is getting too thin, feed a little more. You can feed him all the hay he will eat without hurting him.

Horses are creatures of habit and like to be fed at the same time each day—preferably twice a day. They probably will use the feed more efficiently if you follow a regular schedule. At any rate, they will be more contented and do less damage to your pasture, fences, and stable if you always feed on schedule.

Feed supplements

Every horse magazine contains advertisements for a variety of mineral and vitamin supplements for horses. Some suburban horsemen go "powder happy," thinking they will risk the poor animal's life if they do not feed minerals and vitamins. The cost can be considerable. If you have good green hay or good pasture (fresh succulent grass) and buy grain from a reputable feed company, you probably will not need any supplements. If your hay or pasture is of low quality, however, chances are that you may need to feed a supplement. Also, your particular horse may have special nutritional needs requiring a supplement. If your horse is working hard and if you are after the best performance in shows, you may be willing to pay the added cost on the chance that there may be some benefit. At any rate, if you feed the supplement at the recommended rates and in the recommended way it is not likely to hurt him, even if he does not need it.

Dangers of overfeeding

Beware of overfeeding grain or feeding grain when the horse is hot from hard work. These practices can produce very serious illness from which your horse may not recover, or result in his reduced usefulness for the rest of his life. A regular amount at each feeding is the rule to follow. Let him cool off after hard work before he is fed, and also avoid hard work immediately after he is fed grain. To stop a horse from bolting his grain, many horsemen feed hay first to take the edge off a horse's hunger, then dole out grain.

If your horse gets into the grain supply and eats freely, he surely will overeat. When excessive amounts of grain are consumed, the fermentation of the grain releases gases in large quantities. This will cause serious trouble. If this happens, *consult your vet* right away.

You can have a similar problem if your horse gets out and finds an apple tree from which he can eat apples freely. He will not know when to stop, and he may have a serious case of the colic if he eats too many. If the horse acts restless, swells in the flanks and stomach, or tries to roll and bite at his sides, call the vet.

These situations are also thought to contribute to the development of a condition known as "founder" or "laminitis," an inflammation of the sensitive layers of tissue in the hoof. The causes of this condition are not well understood by veterinarians. A horse with founder is lame in all four feet. The feet are feverish, and the shape of the sole of the hoof changes from concave to convex in advanced stages of the condition. If your horse walks as if all his feet are sore, call the vet right away.

There are plants a horse shouldn't eat. In the eastern United States, wild cherry trees are numerous. The leaves of those trees are poisonous when they are wilted, and if the horse eats them it may kill him or cause severe colic. In your area there may be other plants poisonous to horses. This is another item to check with your vet.

Water

Your horse should have a supply of clean water available to him at all times or provided at regular intervals. Keep his water container clean. Carrying water to horses can become one of the more onerous chores, so some form of automatic watering device is recommended. At least have a faucet or hose conveniently located to make the chore easier. In Chapter 7 we tell you more about how you can arrange it.

Exercise

Your horse, like you, needs exercise. You cannot expect him to stand in a stall for a couple of weeks and then on a nice day take you for a long ride. If you keep him in a pasture, he will get enough exercise to keep in fairly good condition. However, even then, if you expect him to take you on long weekend rides or do his best in a weekend show, he should have more exercise. A little riding or a few minutes on a longe line (a line about 30 feet long) every other day will help to keep him in good condition.

Longeing teaches obedience to young horses and is good exercise for any horse. Buckle the longe line to the noseband of the halter and start the horse around, getting him to change gaits by voice command. Don't forget a reward for good performance.

Parasite control

Anyone whose horses are confined in a small area must be concerned about the control of internal parasites, especially in humid climates where nature is kind to the parasites during that part of their life cycle when they are outside the horse.

Once parasites are established in a pasture, they become part of a self-sustaining cycle, passing through the horse to the ground and back to the horse as he grazes.

There are several kinds of parasites to control. They have several characteristics in common. Part of their life cycle is spent outside the horse and the remainder is in the horse's digestive system or other parts of his body. They live off the feed the horse consumes or off the horse's body itself, and do considerable damage to his vital organs. Parasites reduce the efficiency with which the horse uses his feed. They cause or contribute to a variety of illnesses, cause the horse to lack energy and spirit, make him generally unhealthy and run down, or directly cause the horse's death in extreme cases. The major internal parasites are these:

Bots. In late summer or early fall you may notice small yellow specks on the legs of your horse. These are botfly eggs. From the legs they get in the horse's mouth as he bites or scratches his legs. In the mouth they hatch and work their way to the stomach where they spend the winter in the larvae stage (about 1 inch long). The next summer they pass to the ground to emerge as flies to lay more eggs. While in the stomach they attach to the stomach wall and may cause considerable damage, including colic and generally unthrifty conditions.

Ascarids. The ascarid, a worm 6 to 12 inches long, inhabits the horse's intestines. It lays eggs that pass to the ground and are picked up by the horse as he eats. They hatch, migrate through the body tissues, and eventually end up in the intestines again. Ascarids cause digestive disturbances and other illnesses as they migrate through lungs, the heart, and other organs.

Strongyles. These are worms up to about 2½ inches long. When mature they inhabit the intestines and lay eggs that pass to the ground. There the eggs hatch and the larvae climb stems of the grass. They are swallowed by the horse as he feeds. In the body they migrate through body tissues and end up in the intestines. They can cause serious illness, including diarrhea and general debility.

Pinworms. Pinworms are 3 to 6 inches long, found in the intestines. They lay eggs that pass from the horse and are picked up as he eats. Pinworms cause an irritation of the anus that makes the horse rub his tail on fences and trees. Pinworms can cause serious illness as well.

No matter where you keep your horse or how you care for him he probably will have some parasites at times, but if he is kept in a restricted area you must do constant battle. You should consult a veterinarian, your County Agent, or other expert on methods of parasite control suitable for your situation and develop a program of control.

Generally the recommended systems of control include such items as these:

1. Rotate pastures to break up the cycle. Use a field for pasture one year and for hay or cultivated crops the next.

2. Don't let horses drink from streams or ponds in the pasture.

3. Break up piles of manure in the pasture and spread them frequently.

4. Don't spread stable manure on the pasture.

5. Pile manure so the heat caused by decay can kill the parasite eggs, before using it for any purpose.

6. Clean stables daily and don't use bedding material that horses can eat.

7. Never feed hay on the floor of the stall or on the ground.

8. In paddocks with closely confined horses, pick up the manure and remove it from the paddock.

10. Use worm medicines as recommended by your veterinarian.

If you are a suburban horseman, you may not be able to follow suggestion 1, and you may need to compromise with other practices. Your situation probably will require frequent use of worm medicine. Start fighting parasites as soon as you get a horse and keep it up. Don't wait until you have a horse who obviously is suffering. If you attend to this problem from the start, it probably never will become serious and you will enjoy your horses much more.

I have my veterinarian worm my horses in the spring and in

the fall; and once in winter and once in summer I put worm medicine in their feed.

At most tack shops and feedstores you can buy worm medicines to mix with grain. Different medicines contain certain chemicals that vary in their effectiveness against the several parasites. You should select one that is effective against the parasites your horse is most likely to have—and choose a medicine your horse will eat.

Administering worm medicine in the feed is not fully satisfactory. Generally horses are able to smell or taste the medicine. If your horse eats only part of the feed he may not consume enough of the medicine to do the job. If he does not eat the grain at all you have wasted the medicine and the grain. Some say that if you let the horse get quite hungry before feeding the grain and medicine you increase the chances that the horse will eat it all. Others suggest that before feeding the medicine you put Vicks Vapor Rub up each nostril of the horse. The Vicks is supposed to confuse the horse's sense of smell so that he will eat the mixture.

I had one horse who would not eat grain with medicine no matter how hungry she was, and Vicks did not fool her a bit. When we tried to add medicine to her grain, she refused to eat grain for several days.

If your horse is equally adamant about worm medicine, your veterinarian can run a tube through a nostril and down to the stomach. He then pours or pumps a liquid medicine down the tube. This way he can use the most effective chemicals, he knows it all reaches the stomach, and he can use just the right amount for your horse. If you have the veterinarian do the job when he is there for other purposes, it will not cost much more for him to worm the horses than for you to do it through the feed, and you will be sure the horses receive the right medicine in the right dosage.

Here is another idea that may help you. In some communities horse owners organize a "worming day." They arrange for a veterinarian to be at a central location, and each owner takes his horse there. The vet is kept busy treating one horse after another. The cost is less than when the vet has to make a house call for each horse, and the vet saves valuable time.

Disease control

Horses are subject to a number of serious diseases. Fortunately, vaccines are available to protect your horse against many of them. To be fully effective, some of these vaccines should be administered annually. Others require booster shots. You should consult your veterinarian about the shots he recommends for your area. Also consider the use you make of your horse. The more your horse is around strange horses and the more you take him to public stables or other facilities, the more you need to protect him against communicable diseases.

Tetanus (lockjaw) is one disease against which you certainly want protection. This is the same disease as the tetanus against which you and your family are immunized. It is as disastrous a disease for a horse as it is for a person: if untreated, it means almost certain death. Since horses are particularly prone to wounds that usually occur under rather dirty circumstances, the hazard and the need for immunization are high.

Shipping fever, or influenza, is a very contagious respiratory disease. It is very common around some sale facilities, hence its name.

Several years ago I bought a pony an an auction, brought him home, and released him. The kids affectionately named him Horace. About two weeks later Horace developed a bad cough, with a very high temperature and a heavy yellow nasal discharge. Penicillin shots solved the problem, but two weeks later another horse came down with it, and then another. About $150 worth of vet bills later we had them all cured. I can assure you that my horses have had influenza shots annually from then on. Learn from my experience, please. The second lesson from my experience is this: Keep a new horse separate until he has time to develop any contagious disease to which he may have been exposed.

There are three strains of sleeping sickness—Eastern, Western, and Venezuelan. You may recall that about 1970 the Venezuelan strain entered this country from Mexico. It is not now present in this country but might return and spread rapidly. Outbreaks of Eastern and Western sleeping sickness occur frequently. Before vaccinating your horse, consult your vet about the hazard in your area. You now can use one vaccine that immunizes for all three strains. You might as well use this and have immunity from three diseases for the price of one.

Swamp fever, or equine infectious anemia, is another contagious disease of concern to most horsemen. It is spread by biting insects and the use of unsterile medical equipment, bits, and so on. A high proportion of infected animals die. The survivors remain carriers for life. There is no known cure, nor a means of immunizing, but there is a blood test to detect carriers. Some states now require tests of horses entering the state. Many fairs, shows, and sales require a Coggins Test of all horses in attendance. This is a growing practice and an effective way to avoid exposure and limit the spread of the disease. If you buy a horse, consider giving him a Coggins Test before closing the deal.

Distemper is another fairly common contagious disease. The symptoms are about like distemper in cats and dogs. In addition to a cough and nasal discharge the infected animal is likely to develop an abscess in the glands between the jaws. This may break and drain or have to be lanced. Fortunately, immunization is possible. Check with the vet on the hazard in your area.

Another common illness is colic. This is not a disease caused by a germ or virus and therefore immunization is not possible. The term "colic" is generally used to refer to stomach pains that may be due to any one of a number of causes. If your horse should be in pain, have contracted abdominal muscles, lay down and roll frequently, or bite his sides, he probably has colic. It can be fatal. Call the vet right away. Until he gets there keep the horse walking—for the most common types of colic this may bring him out of the trouble, or it may help avoid worse problems.

If you have a horse who contracts lockjaw, sleeping sickness, shipping fever, or some other serious disease, you will decide very quickly that the cost of annual shots is small indeed compared with his having such a disease. As a minimum, you should give him a tetanus shot each year, but consult your veterinarian. He will charge you somewhere between $3 and $10 for each shot.

Preventive medicine

Schedule shots and worm medicine to be given at some special time—for example, when you turn the horses into the pasture in the spring, or after the first killing frost in the fall. These are particularly good times. In the spring you will be giving the shots just ahead of the season when you are most likely to be taking your horse places where he might be exposed to disease. If you worm him just ahead of being turned out to pasture, he will drop a minimum of parasite eggs that could reinfect him. After frost in the fall is a good time to rid him of bots, a parasite he is likely to have picked up during late summer and early fall.

If you have one or more horses and add another, be careful that the newcomer does not bring diseases to infect the others. Be especially careful if the new horse was purchased at an auction or from a dealer who has many horses coming and going through his stables. It is a good idea to keep such a horse separate from the others for two or three weeks so that any disease to which he may have been exposed has a chance to develop. Consult your veterinarian about other precautions.

The cost of preventive medicine is one you should not try to

Checking for windpuffs, or windgalls, soft swellings above the fetlock joint. Windpuffs usually are not painful to the horse.

avoid—to do so is false economy. The rules of preventive medicine in horses are about like those for people. Vaccinate to prevent diseases whenever possible. Avoid unnecessary exposure to disease. Keep horses well nourished to help fight diseases that strike. Cleanliness—in stalls, feedboxes, and water supply—is essential. Have a separate bit for each horse. Use disposable hypodermic needles.

Frequently the teeth with which a horse chews—those on the back of the jaws—develop rough edges that irritate him when he eats. When this happens he doesn't chew his feed well and he may not eat as much as he needs. When the vet is there have him check the teeth and "float" them if they need it. Floating consists of using a special file to round off the sharp edges.

You may wonder how you will know when your horse is sick. Of course if he isn't acting normally you will suspect that something is wrong. If he is in pain he may stand with his head hanging so his nose nearly touches the ground. He may groan like a person in pain. If he has stomach pains his abdomen will seem to be drawn up and the abdominal muscles will be contracted and conspicuous. If he stands with nostrils widely dilated, this may also indicate pain. He may be breathing rapidly; he may have a fever and feel hot to the touch. The vet takes a horse's temperature with a special rectal thermometer. (You probably will not have enough need to justify buying one.) If he has other symptoms and feels hot, call the vet. If he is lying down, will not get up, and has some of these symptoms, *call the vet quickly.*

Avoiding injuries

We strongly urge you to notice features of your stable, fences, and equipment on which your horse could be injured. (For details, see Chapter 7.) This is most important if you want to keep the doctor bills low, for when your horse is injured the probability of infection is very high, almost a certainty. Apply an appropriate medicine immediately to any cut. If the cut is deep, the horse probably will need an antibiotic to help fight the infection. For such cuts, call your veterinarian—at least until you have acquired enough experience and medicine to be sure you can take care of it.

No matter how diligently you try to prevent it, your horse will need some doctoring from time to time. You can save a lot of money by learning to do some of it yourself. When your veterinarian prescribes shots of an antibiotic, he probably will be glad to teach you how to give the shots. Most veterinarians are very helpful in teaching horse owners to administer medicines and first aid. You might become quite expert at recognizing simple problems that you can treat yourself.

Use of blankets

Of all the practices used by recreational horse owners, probably placing blankets on horses is the most overdone. If your horse develops a normal winter coat, he usually does not need a blanket. Of course, if you work him so hard on a cold winter day that he is wet, then a blanket for a short time until he dries off is a good idea.

Wearing a blanket continuously causes a horse to shed his winter coat. If you are entering him in a show or sale you may want him in that condition, but then you will have to be careful because he will no longer have his natural protection against the cold. He will be better off in a natural condition and can face the coldest of winter nights without any blanket.

If you haul your horse in a trailer on a cold day, the added protection of a blanket may be desirable, depending on how much protection your trailer provides.

But when you have an especially cold night don't rush out and put a blanket on your horse. Doing so will be no favor to him.

Washing and grooming

While we are on the subject of overdone practices, let's discuss horse washing.

In a state of nature, horses get washed incidentally when caught in a rain without protection or if they are forced to swim a river. Otherwise they get along very well without it. No problems result from the lack of a bath. This is also true of domesticated horses.

On returning from a hard drive with a horse wet with sweat, some people like to hose him down with cold water. How would you like to have someone do that to you, especially in the winter? Washing with cold water when a horse is hot or the weather is cold is a severe shock. Furthermore, the use of soap and detergents removes natural oils from the skin and hair.

Instead, after a hard ride, walk the horse slowly until he dries off, then brush him.

About the only time it is necessary to wash a horse is when he is to be in a show, when you don't want a gray who looks dusty yellow. If you must wash him, scrape off the excess water and let him dry in a place where he will not be exposed to cold winds.

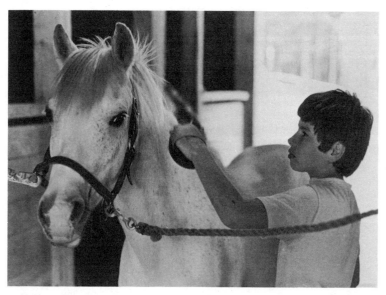

Vigorous swirling strokes with the currycomb will remove caked-on dirt and loose hair. Cross-tie your horse before grooming.

The best way to get a horse clean is with a brush and plenty of "elbow grease." You may enjoy brushing your horse, and he will probably enjoy it, too. Give him all the attention he wants. On the other hand, this is a job that does not need to take much time, if it is a chore for you. If you are not using him, he can be turned out to pasture all winter without any brushing.

He should always be brushed before you put the saddle on, and after you return from a ride—particularly paying attention to the parts of the body where the saddle fits. If you want your horse to look his best and if you enjoy compliments on his beauty, give him a good vigorous brushing frequently.

Hoof care

Your horse's feet require attention. If he is kept under ideal conditions (in a pasture that is not muddy), the attention required will be minimal. If he is kept in a stall or in dirty, wet, or muddy circumstances, you should pick the dirt out of his hoofs frequently. Some recommend doing this daily, but once a week may suffice. Horses are prone to a decay of the hoof called "thrush." If the decay is there you will notice a vile odor when you clean the hoof. At your feedstore or tack shop you can get a medicine to apply to the hoof easily to overcome the problem. Keep the horse on dry ground if possible.

A horse's hoofs grow at the rate of about a quarter of an inch a month. If he is in a paddock or pasture where he can run and if you ride him sometimes, his hoofs probably will wear off at about the same rate as they grow. If you keep him in a stall and do not use him much, you will need to trim his hoofs about once every month or six weeks. If he is kept where his hoofs wear down, they may not wear evenly and you may need to trim them occasionally to make them even—the same height on each side, and proper height on heel and toe.

Trimming a horse's hoofs is not a particularly difficult job, once he learns to hold his foot up for you. If he lets you hold the weight of the foot and then leans on you a little to boot, it can be hard work. The tools required are inexpensive. An experienced horseman or farrier can teach you to do the job very quickly.

First you need to learn to pick up the feet in such a way that the horse will help you and to avoid the chances of being stepped on or kicked. If the horse has spent a long time without much attention to his feet, you may need to handle his feet frequently just to get him accustomed to having you work on them. When you are buying a horse, it is a good idea to find out how he feels about having his feet handled by a "greenhorn" or a stranger.

Some suburbanites think that their horses must have shoes. Remember, in the wild no horses had shoes. It is best to keep your horse barefoot if you can. If he does not wear his hoofs down too much in the pasture, and if you do not use him much on paved roads and other places where his hoofs wear rapidly, he probably will not need shoes. Some horses need shoes only on the front feet, where a greater part of the weight of the horse and rider is carried.

Use a hoof pick to clean dirt and pebbles from your horse's feet. Smell each hoof to detect early signs of thrush, a decay of the frog caused by unsanitary conditions.

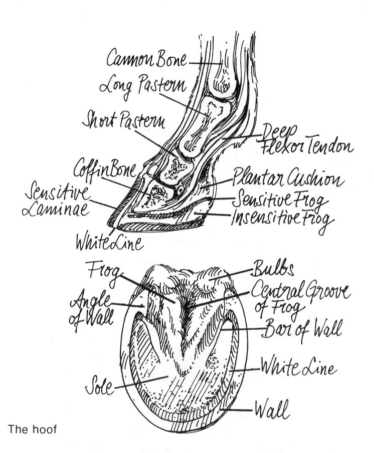

Cannon Bone
Long Pastern
Short Pastern
Deep Flexor Tendon
Coffin Bone
Plantar Cushion
Sensitive Laminae
Sensitive Frog
Insensitive Frog
White Line

Frog
Bulbs
Angle of Wall
Central Groove of Frog
Bar of Wall
White Line
Sole
Wall

The hoof

Keeping your horse barefoot avoids the cost of shoeing, the necessity to remember to have him shod about every six to eight weeks, and foot problems that may result from poorly fitting shoes and shoes left on too long.

On the other hand, some horses need shoes for other reasons—they have hoofs that break off easily or crack if not shod, or they have abnormalities in the feet or in the way they travel that require corrective shoeing, just as some people require corrective shoes. You may want your horse shod if you plan to use him in activities that involve a high probability of hoof damage.

In most communities, there are farriers who travel from

place to place taking care of horses' feet and carrying the necessary supplies and equipment with them. The horsemen in your community can tell you who they are. You can learn to shoe your own horse but you probably will not want to do so for only one or a small number of horses. If you do want to learn, ask your County Agent where you can obtain the training. After watching a farrier shoe a stubbon horse who does not want to be shod, you are almost sure to decide to let someone else do this job.

Putting a horse down

An unpleasant subject, but one many of us have to face at some point, is the difficult task of "putting a horse down" (killing him humanely). This is sometimes necessary. If a horse has swamp fever, government regulations require that he be quarantined under conditions that would be prohibitively costly for a recreation horse owner—so putting him down can be the only realistic alternative. A broken leg sometimes can be mended but the horse has to be kept immobile for a long time at great expense. Some broken legs cannot be repaired.

If you have to put a horse away you have to consider your family as well as the horse. Probably you will want to have the vet do it in a very humane way, usually by an injection. (There are other ways to destroy a horse—including shooting, if you are a good shot.) You may want to plan for the vet to do the job when young members of your family are away—or maybe not, but don't forget the psychological impact on them. You may be able to bury the body at home, but your local health department may prohibit this (check with them). You may prefer to have the body disposed of by someone else. There probably is a rendering company or dog-food plant that will pick it up, *if* this is a satisfactory solution for you and your family.

♞ 6

Horse equipment

Selecting a saddle

As soon as you get your horse, you will be tempted to hurry out and buy a saddle. Unless you have had enough experience to know for sure what you want, you should take time to decide what saddle best suits you and your needs.

Saddles come in many styles, sizes, and qualities—and at a wide range of prices. The saddle you get should be selected for the use you plan to make of the horse. It should fit you, your horse, and your pocketbook. So great is the variety of saddles available that you should be able to find one to meet all of your requirements.

You may plan to use your horse in a combination of ways that will require two or more saddles (for example, jumping and pleasure riding), but don't buy more saddles than you need.

The two basic types of saddles are English and Western, and there are many variations in each. If you plan to use your horse only for pleasure riding, either an English or Western saddle will serve your needs. You may feel more secure or comfortable on a Western saddle and buy one for that reason. Or you may prefer an English saddle because there will be less material between you and the horse and this will make communication with the horse easier.

ENGLISH SADDLE

Pommel

Seat

Cantle

Skirt

Stirrup Bar

Panel

Stirrup Iron

Flap

Stirrup Leather

Horn

Fork

Cantle

Pommel

Seat

Skirt

Wool Lining

Back Housing

Skirt

Fender

Girth

Front Tie Strap, or Cinch Strap

Stirrup

WESTERN SADDLE

If you expect to jump with your horse, you will want an English saddle designed for jumping. These saddles make it easy to assume the proper jumping position, and they help the rider grip the horse with his knees when going over jumps. If you plan to go in for dressage you may get along with any type of English saddle for a while. But eventually, if you stay with it, you will want a special dressage saddle. It reduces to a minimum the amount of material that interferes with communication between your body and the horse. For certain show events, you may need a "flat" English saddle, and you may even want a sidesaddle.

Similarly, Western saddles have various designs for special uses, enabling the rider or the horse to do certain jobs with more ease or comfort. For example, if you plan to use your horse in cutting competition, you may want a saddle designed especially for this. You should become acquainted with a number of features of Western saddle design and construction before making your selection.

Western saddles frequently are decorated with extensive carving, stitching, and other decorations. These features add considerably to the cost. It is not necessary to buy an extensively decorated saddle to get high quality in materials and construction.

Both English and Western saddles come in several sizes. You should have one that is comfortable and safe for you and your horse.

Prices of both English and Western saddles vary greatly, and so does the quality associated with the differences in price. In the case of saddles, a less expensive model can serve the needs of most of us quite well, but be certain to examine a saddle closely. Consider comfort, durability, ease of care, safety, and appearance. The parts that hold the saddle to the horse and the parts that connect the stirrups to the saddle are the most important safety features. The girth and stirrup leathers should be thick and of high quality. Frequently the girth (the part going around the horse's belly and fastened to the saddle on both sides) is bought separately from the saddle.

The most expensive English-style saddles are made in Europe. You will find similar South American saddles, some almost carbon copies, that are well-made and durable and sell for much less than their European counterparts. Some of the lower-priced saddles are made of lower-quality leather—but leather that still is quite durable and serviceable.

English saddles made in Argentina retail in the $100–$200 range, while saddles made in Great Britain or other European countries are in the area of $250-$500. To check on prices a little more you might order Sears Roebuck's special Farm and Ranch Catalogue, which includes a variety of horse equipment.

You may be able to buy a good used saddle for half the price of a new one. In your area there probably are tack shops with used saddles. Also, at some horse auctions used tack is sold. (Be sure to examine any used equipment before the sale starts.)

If you buy a used saddle, you should especially be interested in the wear and deterioration that has taken place in the leather and other parts. Be sure the tree (wood or metal framework of the saddle) is not broken. If you place the saddle on a flat surface and push down on it, the body of the saddle should be as rigid as a new one. Also check to be sure the stirrup leathers and the parts that connect the saddle to the girth are not badly worn or deteriorated.

Selecting a bridle

The bridle, which includes reins, bit, head straps, and throatlatch, also comes in two general styles, English and Western. If you ride in a show, you may prefer a bridle and saddle of the same type, but there is no law of nature or man that says you can't mix them when riding for pleasure. (Your

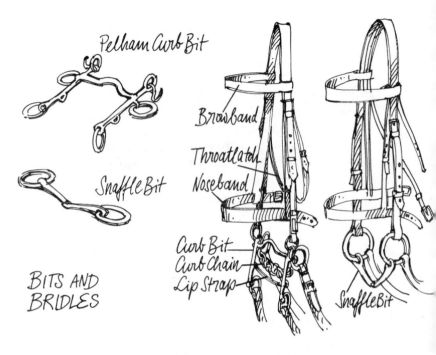

Pelham Curb Bit

Snaffle Bit

Browband

Throatlatch

Noseband

Curb Bit
Curb Chain
Lip Strap

Snaffle Bit

BITS AND
BRIDLES

friends may think something is wrong with you, but the horse
will not know the difference.) Both styles vary in design; the
one you use is entirely a matter of personal preference.

There are many price and quality variables among bridles,
too. Generally, better bridles are made of thick, pliable leather
and strong metal parts. They also have stitching where pieces
of leather are joined and along the edges of the leather.

Bits

The variety of bits available is very large, with hundreds of
different designs and sizes. You can find many articles in horse
publications discussing the suitability of various bits.

The purpose of a bit is to help you communicate with your
horse. If the rider and horse are well acquainted, the rider may
be able to communicate sufficiently with just a halter and rope.
Instead of a bit, a "bosal" (or hackamore) is sometimes used.

This is a rather stiff, rope-like piece that surrounds the horse's nose and is attached to the reins. Some horses are trained for use of the bosal, and some horses and horsemen prefer it to a bit. But most people, especially beginners, use a bit and reins.

The beginning horseman should be acquainted with two major characteristics that are different from one bit to another. One is the diameter of the piece that goes through the horse's mouth: the smaller the diameter of this piece, the more severe is its effect on the horse's jaw.

At a pony club meeting, an instructor shows a young horseman how to make sure the bit and bridle are correctly fitted. Allow two fingers' space under the throatlatch and the noseband, and be sure the bit is the right width for the horse's mouth.

Bits also differ in the amount of leverage exerted by pulling on the reins. Snaffle bits have a ring on each end of the mouthpiece to which the reins are attached. You pull directly on the bit, exerting little pressure on the horse's mouth. A curb bit, on the other hand, is anchored by a chain and gives the rider considerable leverage by putting severe pressure on the mouth.

I mention these two features of bits because a rider lacking in skill and training, if using one of the more severe bits, can unknowingly cause a horse great pain and do serious damage to the animal's mouth.

The kind of bit you should use depends on your skill as a rider, the training and disposition of the horse, the sensitivity of the horse's mouth, and the use you are making of him. If your horse has been trained and used only with a snaffle bit, you probably should use a snaffle, at least until you find need for another. If he is accustomed to a curb bit, perhaps you should start out with a similar bit, but most likely you will need nothing more severe than a snaffle if you are going to use him for pleasure riding.

You may need to try several bits before you find the one that suits you and your horse best. There are many variations between the extremes of snaffle and curb. It's best to start with the kind of bit the previous owner used. Be sure your bit is the right size for the horse. When the bit is in his mouth, the pieces on the end should not be tight up against his face, nor should they stick out.

Halters

You will need at least one halter, primarily for leading and tying your horse. Rope halters and nylon halters are very strong, almost unbreakable, and inexpensive. Even if you need a more expensive decorative halter for exhibiting the horse in shows, you probably will want a nylon or rope halter to use when the horse is tied.

Saddle soap, water, and elbow grease keeps tack soft and supple and prolongs its life. Repair or replace worn straps and girths.

If you are going to haul the horse or tie him for some time, by all means use a halter and rope that are not likely to break. Most horses have learned that when they are haltered and tied there is no use fighting it, and they stand patiently. A horse may be startled and try to get free. If he succeeds, it can be dangerous, but more importantly, he has learned that he can do it. This is one lesson you do not want your horse to learn, so don't tie him with equipment he can break.

Other equipment

You will want one or more lead lines. Almost any kind of line is satisfactory for leading your horse, but if you are going to use the line to tie him, have a good one. Nylon lines are very strong, but beware of the metal snap. Some very strong lines have a flimsy snap that will break the first time the horse puts a little weight against it. If you are going to tie the horse, it is best to tie the rope directly to the halter. When tying your horse in a trailer, use a special safety snap designed so you can release the horse even if he is pulling on the rope.

You will need some other inexpensive items of equipment: saddle pad, brush, currycomb, hoof pick, shedding comb, clippers, twitch, and other things. Get them as you find a need for them. There is almost no limit to the gear and gadgets you can add to your collection. They will make good Christmas presents for you and your horse. The total cost of a brush, hoof pick, currycomb, and saddle pad (minimum needs) should not exceed $25.

There is a variety of other specialized equipment that might interest you: special reins to help train a horse to hold his head at a desired angle, a special harness to train a young horse to drive, padding to protect the legs while hauling the horse in a trailer, horse bandages, hobbles, and so on. For an easy way to learn about what's available and get an idea of costs, consult the Sears Roebuck Farm and Ranch Catalogue mentioned earlier.

Buying a trailer: costs and considerations

You probably will want to haul your horse occasionally—to shows, to some distant place to ride, to a stud farm, or perhaps to a special veterinarian. If you own a trailer you can go and come as you please.

However, it is impractical to own a trailer only for infrequent hauling. If you are going to haul the horse no more than three or four times a year, it will be cheaper to hire or rent a trailer than to own one, even over a number of years. Someone in your neighborhood probably will haul your horse for a small fee, or you can rent a trailer and the necessary hitch for your car.

When you consider buying a trailer, be sure to figure the costs

All the paraphernalia necessary for a horse show: a four-wheeled, two-horse trailer with front escape door, pulled by a pick-up truck with room for tack and other equipment.

that go along with it. You will need a sturdy hitch on your car. You may be pulling, and at times be pushed by, 2,000 pounds of trailer and 2,000 pounds of horse, a considerable load. Don't take chances on a questionable hitch to save a few dollars; it could be very costly in the end.

Don't overlook the cost of connecting the car's braking system to the trailer brakes and the car's lights to the trailer lights. Most states require horse trailers to have lights and brakes. Even if your state does not require them, don't take the risks of driving without them.

You should use a heavy car or pick-up truck to pull a trailer safely, especially if you travel on open highways and in hilly areas. Costs of gas, oil, and wear and tear on your car and trailer may be more than the cost of hiring someone to haul the trailer.

But if you do decide to buy a trailer, you'll find they come in a wide range of prices and with a variety of special features. Buying one is about like buying a car.

You can buy a basic model, or you can buy a trailer that has an escape door to enable you to leave from the front after you lead the horse in from the rear (a very desirable feature), various amounts of padding wherever the horse comes in contact with the wood or metal, tack and feed compartments, a closet for dressing or changing clothes, a small living compartment to use while on the road with the horse, and many more features. The trailer you buy depends, of course, on your needs as well as on your ability to pay. If you are going to spend large amounts of time going to distant horse shows, you may want a more elaborate rig than you will need for an occasional local trip.

Your state probably has safety laws applying to horse trailers and perhaps to the towing vehicles. Be sure to check these laws before you buy. Whether or not your state requires it, I strongly recommend a four-wheeled trailer with brakes on two of the wheels. If you have a blowout at high speed, a two-wheeled trailer is much more difficult to handle than a four-wheeled trailer, particularly with a horse shifting his weight as he tries to stay on his feet. There are other advantages to a four-wheeled trailer, but this one is enough if you are likely to be traveling on main roads and at speeds other cars are traveling.

Good trailer brakes are a must for safety if you are going any distance on main roads. If your car weighs 4,000 pounds and you are pulling a 4,000-pound load, you have twice the weight your car brakes were designed to stop. Without trailer brakes you may be all right as long as you have plenty of space to slow down and you drive on fairly level roads. But if the car ahead stops suddenly, a child darts into the road, or some other unexpected situation develops, you will need extra braking power to go with the extra load. Slippery or gravelly road surfaces increase the need for trailer brakes. Be sure to have them properly adjusted for the load in the trailer.

Used trailers do not depreciate rapidly if they are kept in good condition, and you may be able to save considerable money by buying one. Some probably are available in your area. If you buy a used one, check the condition of the brakes, hitch, lights, tires, and other obvious features.

Don't overlook the trailer floor, which is usually made of wood. Many trailers are kept outdoors where rain and snow can blow inside freely. The floor may be covered with a rubber pad and perhaps an accumulation of straw and manure. Under such conditions, wood can decay rapidly, depending on the climate, the kind of wood used, and any protective treatment given the wood before it was installed. Check the condition of the floor boards, looking for signs of decay. You do not want your horse to break through the floor while you are driving happily down the interstate highway. This caution applies also if you own a new trailer. Clean it out after you use it and keep it where the floor will remain dry. Check the condition of the floor boards at least yearly.

Before buying a trailer, study the features of the various brands. Talk with other trailer owners to help decide which is best for you, your horse, and your needs.

The tack and equipment you buy will have much to do with your enjoyment and safety in owning and using a horse. The items included here are only the essentials, and I've discussed only some of their basic features. As long as you have a horse you will continue to learn about and want additional items, most of which are optional if you want to keep your costs down.

♞ 7
Sensible facilities for your horse

You may have in mind a beautiful rural vista with white fences, red barns, and colts playing knee-deep in beautiful bluegrass. It is a good objective, but on a small piece of ground in a community with close neighbors you probably will not be able to recreate that scene.

At least you will want your place to be attractive, an asset to your community, a place you and your neighbors are proud of. If keeping a horse were to turn your place into an eyesore and a source of flies and undesirable odors, you certainly would not get full enjoyment from your horse hobby.

You need to be aware of some things about a horse as you plan the facilities in which you are going to keep him.

Natural and suburban environments

The natural home of the horse is the wide open spaces, where he roamed in small bands over large areas. He was able to graze a little here and a little there as he went. His body wastes were widely scattered. His main defense against his enemies was his great speed, and at the least hint of danger he bounded away to greater safety. When cornered, he fought viciously by biting and kicking.

Horse facilities on this six-acre homesite include a four-acre fenced pasture with a shelter.

During storms, the herd sought shelter among trees or against a bank of earth or near a cliff. Through thousands of years of natural selection, the horse developed as an animal that thrived on such a life. During the relatively short period since the horse was domesticated, he has not changed much from the wild horse of early history.

The more natural his environment, the less difficulty he has. On a small property you cannot keep him in a truly natural environment, but you can keep the resulting problems to a minimum.

A horse wants to roam and run as in nature. He also wants the companionship and protection provided by the herd. If he is alone he will try to get near other horses; if he's startled, he will try to flee from danger. We have to fence him in and limit his ability to do these things.

If you could turn a small number of horses out in a 100-acre field, there would not be much pressure on the fences and it would not take an elaborate fence to hold them. The more they are restrained, the greater the pressure on the fences. When you have two or three horses in a 1-acre pasture it takes a good fence to hold them. If they are kept in a 50 by 50-foot paddock with green grass on the other side of the fence, one needs a very good fence indeed.

At the approach of winter, the horse grows a heavy coat, and changes take place in his skin to help keep him warm. These provide good natural protection against the cold, but he needs some shelter from storms. A shed enclosed on three sides is sufficient. If he is closed up tightly in a small barn, a most unnatural environment, he is almost certain to suffer from colds and other illness.

During periods of wet weather, especially during the winter, your horse's feet will sink into the ground, turning a small paddock, and perhaps your whole pasture, into one continuous mire of mud.

Horses that are confined get bored, just as you or I would. For something to do, they chew on almost anything. They will chew the bark off most kinds of trees, killing the trees. They probably will chew at the boards on your fences and stable, particularly those that are softwood.

If they can reach through or over the fence, they will eat almost anything on the other side, including your rose bushes and the neighbor's azaleas. They will keep reaching farther and farther, leaning on the fence, until a weak board breaks. When they break out of the fence they may graze contentedly on your lawn—or they may so enjoy their new freedom that they race full speed across the lawns of the community.

Confined horses can become quite expert at opening gates, including "horseproof" locks and hitches. So be prepared.

In the wild, horses ate large quantities of grass and other vegetation. To approximate their natural diet, provide plenty of pasture and hay. In your pasture they will overgraze some areas, pulling the grass out by the roots, and let the grass grow long in other areas because it contains some weeds they don't like to eat. The weeds will grow, reproduce, and reappear in greater numbers next year.

Horses pick up internal parasites from the vegetation they eat. The more manure there is in the pasture, paddock, or stall, the greater this problem will be.

If there is something in their little world they can get hurt on they probably will, sooner or later. Some horses seem to be accident-prone and find the sharp point of a nail in the fence the first day they are in the pasture.

If you do not take into account the nature of the beast, you are likely to have a sickly horse who becomes a community nuisance and makes your place an eyesore. But with sensible planning and care, your horse hobby will be an asset.

Shelter and storage facilities

Local climate conditions or building restrictions may dictate to some extent the kind of shelter you provide and its location on your property.

In addition to providing shelter for the horse, you will need a place to keep saddles, bridles, halters, and medicines. If you are interested in driving horses, an activity of growing popularity, you may need to allow for a sulky and extra tack. You'll also need room for feed and bedding. You may use a complete pelleted feed; in this case, if you make a weekly trip to the feedstore, the storage space needed for feed will be small. You can keep it in the garage or some other place around the house. However, in most areas you can feed a horse just as well at lower cost by feeding hay, with grain when needed.

If you have the space to store a winter's supply of hay, you will save a lot of trouble. Next best would be to have space to store a pickup truckload. It is not difficult to find a farmer who will sell a large quantity of hay at little or no extra cost for delivery. Of course, you may not mind hauling a few bales of hay once a week in the family car. In that case you can save the cost of providing storage space. Most people prefer the convenience of storing hay and bedding in the stable along with the other supplies and tack. If you live in a humid climate, don't store hay on the ground—the bales on the bottom may become moldy and unfit for a horse to eat.

A horse, suddenly finding access to an unlimited supply of grain, is like a kid on Halloween with a bag full of treats. He doesn't know when to stop. A horse can eat enough to cause very serious illness and possibly death. Keep this in mind as you plan your stable, particularly if children will be caring for your horses or if children from the community come and go. It is a good idea to design the stable so that a forgetful person in a hurry cannot possibly let the horses get at the grain supply.

Some horses can be ingenious in this situation. I installed horseproof hooks on stall doors, added springs that automatically closed the stall doors, and stored grain in a feedroom box with a hinged lid that closed when not held open. Still, twice in five years a horse got at the grain supply.

It is generally recommended that the floor in a shed or stable be clay rather than concrete, asphalt, or wood. Clay provides greater comfort and safety for the horse, unless you let it become a mire of mud. If you can, put the stable in an area with good natural drainage. Be sure that water running off the roof runs away from the building, and grade the area so that the earth is higher in and around the building. This way, you will have less trouble with wet stalls.

While clay for the floors is recommended, I have had good experience with stone dust obtained from a stone or sand-and-gravel company. (Ask for stone dust or buckwheat stone, both of which consist of ⅜-inch to sand-size particles of tailings from

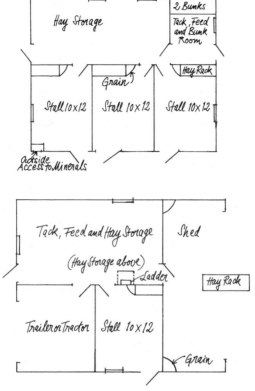

Two stables of the author's own design.

stone-grinding operations.) With this type of floor, water in the stall quickly drains away and it's easy to keep the bedding dry. If you are going to buy stone dust or clay, 2 to 3 cubic yards should be enough for one stall. Of course, people in arid climates and with well-drained soil do not have so serious a problem as those with poorly drained soils in rainy areas.

Plans for small stables can be obtained from your County Agricultural Agent. Plans often include both stalls and storage space, or they can be modified easily by a local builder to suit your special needs. The plans provide enough information so that you or any builder can erect a fine stable. To learn about the various USDA (United States Department of Agriculture) plans, you might order Agricultural Handbook No. 438, *Recreational Buildings and Facilities*, from your County Agent. In your area, prefabricated stables may be available, and there might be a builder who specializes in small horse stables. If you do it yourself, you can build a small stable for less than $1,000 in materials (or, if you can buy used materials, for considerably less). The cost can go up as far as you like.

Construction problems to avoid

The use of oak or other hardwood in the stable will help keep a bored horse from eating his stall. Rough-sawed oak lumber is usually available from local sawmills. There are products on the market for treating wood to keep horses from eating it. You may want to try this approach. It is about your only choice if the stable and fences are made of an easily chewed wood. The softer the wood and the more the horses are confined, the greater is the need to provide some kind of wood treatment. The materials sold for this purpose will not hurt the horse. Some horsemen also try sheathing wood edges with sheet metal—but beware of sharp corners.

As you build the stable, remember a horse's propensity to injure himself. Be doubly sure there are no points of nails sticking through the wood toward the horse—including from the roof, if it is low enough for the horse to reach.

If a horse leans on a board and pushes it loose, nails may be exposed. Fasten any susceptible boards with bolts.

As you build the stable, be careful about dropping nails. A nail in the dirt is likely to end up in your horse's hoof, where it can cause a very painful infection that is difficult to heal.

If there are any glass windows that a horse can reach, cover them with bars or heavy wire. Sometimes the cut ends of wire are sharp as a razor. Look for sharp edges on the ends of fence wire, pieces of metal, or other objects the horse can touch. Avoid all the horse hazards you can. It will save on doctor bills and your anguish over an injured horse.

Appearance counts

You will want to consider how your stable will look on your property and in your neighborhood. For little extra cost you can design the pitch of the roof, the siding, or some other feature of the stable to harmonize with nearby buildings. Where on your property should the stable be placed? To learn of any restrictions, consult your property deed and the local zoning office. You may be required to place it a certain distance from a lot line, and of course you will want to consider the interests of neighbors. These requirements may leave you little alternative. Appearance of your property is an important consideration, but you will also be interested in convenience in doing the chores, providing water, and moving feed and bedding to the stable by truck. Landscaping around the stable is attractive—but then you need to fence the horses away from the trees and shrubs.

Feeding facilities

You will need facilities for feeding grain, hay, minerals, and water. Satisfactory prefabricated hayracks, grain tubs, and drinking fountains are available. Some are designed to be mounted in a corner to conserve stall space.

You can make your own facilities at very low cost. If you build these containers, try to avoid sharp corners and exposed nails on which horses may be injured. We keep a hay rack outside the stable so the horses can eat freely when confined in the paddock.

A mare and her foal will eat grain out of the same tub, but this is about the only time you will see two horses do so. If you do not feed grain to each horse in his stall, the best way to control the amount each gets is to have a separate feed tub for each horse, spaced 10 feet or more apart in the paddock. Even then, some horses may steal from others, so you may need to feed them in stalls or tie them outside until they finish their

Hay Feeding Rack

This slatted hay rack can easily be built against the side of a stall. Be sure it's low enough so a horse lying down cannot get his legs caught under it.

grain. But, unless there is a great difference among your horses in the grain they need, this should not be necessary.

Several horses will eat hay out of the same hay rack if the rack is large enough to allow some space between them. Do not feed hay on the ground. This wastes feed and makes parasite control more difficult.

Feeding supplementary minerals may be necessary if you don't use pellets or grain that have added minerals. A place to feed minerals where they will not get wet may be needed. With a little ingenuity you can build a satisfactory device. I cut a hole about a foot square in the side of my stable and built a mineral container on the inside so the horses could reach through to help themselves to the mineral from the outside.

All horses need salt, usually 1 to 2 ounces a day (and extra in summer when horses lose more salt through sweating). Salt can be mixed in with the grain or set out in blocks. It's best to put a salt "lick" in a container so the horse will not bite off large chunks. Mineralized salt blocks, containing salt, iodine, cobalt, magnesium, and other minerals, satisfy the needs of most horses.

Clean water

If you are lucky you may have a small stream flowing across your pasture, but this probably will not serve the horses' needs when they are confined. Also, drinking from a stream, although convenient, can contribute to parasite and disease problems, particularly if neighbors upstream also have horses.

Your horses should have fresh clean water. You can give them water in pails hung in the corner of the stalls or in a trough in the paddock. You can carry their water from the house, or use a garden hose when the weather is not too cold. The ultimate solution, in convenience if not cost, is to pipe water to the stable and the pasture and to use automatic drinking fountains. If you install heated, nonfreezing drinking fountains, be sure the electric wires are installed so that a bored and curious horse cannot chew them and electrocute himself. Also, check the automatic devices occasionally to be sure they work properly. If you use watering troughs, drinking fountains, or pails, wash them frequently and don't expect the horse to drink stale, stagnant water.

Pasture

You can have fairly good pasture with one horse per acre of land, if you are in a good grass-growing area and give it proper attention.

The first consideration is the kind of grass to plant. Your County Agricultural Agent will have the information you need to decide on the grass to use. Some grasses grow well in hot weather, some in cool. They vary in their nutritive qualities, in the climate and soil types they prefer, and in other ways. Good pasture mixtures usually include a few good grasses and a couple of legumes.

The best grass for you is not necessarily the best for a farmer in your area. You will need a grass that grows vigorously in your climate and on your type of soil, is highly nutritious, and withstands heavy horse traffic. You also want a grass that will survive heavy overgrazing and will compete well with the kinds of weeds that will develop in your pasture. A grass with all these characteristics for your area may not exist. If not, you will have to weigh the strengths and weaknesses of available grasses.

I suggest that you lean toward a grass that will survive and grow with heavy traffic and overgrazing. After all, you will have more pasture with a grass that lives and grows than with a very nutritive grass that soon dies. It is a good idea to plant a mixture of two or more grasses and then see which ones survive and produce. In the suburbs of Washington, D. C., I have found orchard grass and Kentucky 31 fescue to be about the best for this purpose. Also, one should not overlook crabgrass as a summer pasture. At least it is green—and it grows.

To plant grass you will have to work up the soil, fertilize, and perhaps apply lime. Your County Agent can tell you what your soil needs.

There probably is some vegetation on your land now. You might start with that and improve the vegetation and its forage production later.

Fences

I hope you have enough space so your horse can be turned out at least part of the time. (Without it, managing a horse will be more demanding.) Of course, the more space the better.

In selecting a fence, be concerned about local regulations,

appearance, cost, the possibility of horses eating prized shrubs through or over the fence, any danger of horses and children being injured by the fence, initial investment and maintenance costs, and, most important, the suitability of the fence to keep your horses at home. If your horses get out, it probably will be when the neighbor's lawns are soft and when traffic is heaviest on nearby roads. It may also be on a day when Dad is away on a business trip, the children are in school, and Mother is at a meeting.

Electric fence

The cheapest fence is a single strand of electric field wire. Once horses have tested it, they will stay away. Posts can be widely spaced and inexpensive. However, electric fence will add little to the appearance of your property. If the regulator is working properly, it will not kill, but it will badly frighten children who touch it. Electric fence probably is not a satisfactory solution on small acreage in a populous community, but for those in less densely settled areas it will serve very well.

Barbed wire fence

The next fence in cost is barbed wire strung on wood or metal posts, using three or more strands of wire. Your children and the neighbors' will climb through the fence and snag their clothes. But this is not the main problem. Barbed wire is a serious hazard to horses.

Once your frightened horse runs through a barbed fence, you will never use it again. The barbs tear the skin and flesh in an irregular pattern, causing injuries that heal very slowly. Some horses will get barbed wire wrapped around a leg and stand patiently waiting for help, but your horse may become frantic and try to pull loose. Of course, you may have a horse of such calm temperament that the risks are low. Most people keeping horses in small enclosures, however, have ruled out barbed wire.

Woven wire fence

The woven-wire fence probably is the next most expensive, and in a number of ways is more satisfactory than electric or barbed wire. The obvious advantage is its safety, since it does not have the damaging barbs. Woven wire consists of several horizontal strands of wire connected by vertical wires. The fencing comes in various heights and with wide or narrow spacing of strands. The fence may be erected with wooden or steel posts.

Woven wire is commonly used and is satisfactory as a horse fence. However, there are some problems. Sometimes a horse will try to get on the other side and paw at the fence. It is easy for him to get a foot through one of the holes. If he becomes startled, he may try to pull away suddenly, pulling the fence apart and doing serious injury to himself. Also, a tall horse will reach over the fence to eat, gradually bending the fence down and perhaps loosening it from the posts or bending steel posts. Thus, some repair and maintenance is required.

This problem frequently is attacked by putting a strand of barbed wire at the top (less desirable because it's still a hazard) or by running one board along the top of the fence. The board can increase the attractiveness of the fence, if the job is done neatly.

Rail fence

Rail fences are one of the more common types on small suburban acreages. They provide an attractive "rustic" appearance that can enhance the value of your property. It is a more expensive fence than others mentioned; however, its cost does not mean that it is more satisfactory than the others. If a two-rail fence is used, the horses are sure to reach through or over it to eat and, before long, break a top rail and escape. Three or four rails are almost essential, but even with three rails the problem may not be eliminated. The suitability of a rail fence depends in part on the kind of wood used. The rails should be made of a wood that is not easily chewed away by the horses. The posts should be made of a decay-resistant wood (cedar or locust is good) or should be pressure-treated against rot.

In my early days as a suburban horse owner, I found a bargain in chestnut rails. In a matter of months, I had to start replacing rails that were broken or chewed away. Later, I replaced them all with new sassafras rails that were almost as hard as iron and nearly indestructible. I had a three-rail fence through which the horses were able to reach—limiting my wife's ability to grow flowers along the fence. So I then nailed woven wire on one side of the rail fence. The result was a very secure fence with low maintenance needs, but with high initial cost.

Post-and-board fence

Post-and-board fences are very common on horse places throughout the country. They generally have four horizontal boards spaced so that a horse cannot reach through to graze. A white board fence is very attractive, frequently adding to the beauty of the community. The boards are seen easily by the horse and respected by him. The material of which the fence is made determines its durability and maintenance needs. Avoid softwoods to keep maintenance costs down. Also, nail the boards on the inside of the posts so a horse leaning against the fence will not push the boards loose so easily.

Other fences

Sometimes horse fences are made of steel pipe with the vertical posts set in concrete. Such fences are used for very small paddocks where the pressure on the fence is great, such as for stallion paddocks, or where cost is not an important consideration. Chain link fences are also sometimes used for horses. A 5-foot chain link fence with posts set in concrete is the ultimate in security and cost, though not the most attractive.

For more information about fences you might want to obtain USDA Farmer's Bulletin No. 2247, *Fences for the Farm and Rural Home.*

Secure gates

A few words about gates may save you some trouble. You will need gates to get horses and equipment in and out of the pasture or paddock. Plan in advance and make the gates wide enough to accommodate a truck.

I once had a small pond on a 2-acre pasture. When a house in the community caught fire, my pond was the most convenient source of water. To get to the water, a fire truck ran over the fence, and the horses quickly seized the opportunity to run away. I spent half the night chasing horses frightened by sirens and flashing lights. The next weekend I built a special gate big enough for fire trucks, and I've been thankful for it on a number of occasions. The cost of a gate is small compared with the inconvenience of having one too small.

Gates, like doors, sometimes are used by forgetful people who do not close them properly. Gates can be built to close automatically. Your County Agricultural Agent should be able to get you plans for building such a gate. You can hang the gate so that its weight causes it to swing shut automatically. But this may not be enough to keep a strong wind from blowing it open

Automatic Gate Closer

if it's not properly latched. You can hang the gate so that it swings only one way—into the pasture—so a horse leaning on it cannot push it open. You can put the fasteners on the outside where it will be more difficult for an imaginative horse to operate them. You can also rig a gate so a rider can open it by pulling on a rope, without dismounting.

You can rig up an automatic closing device. Here is a system you might use. Fasten a rope to the gate, run the rope through a pulley fastened to a post or tree a few feet outside the fence, and on the end of the rope have a weight sufficiently heavy to pull the gate closed. By using a combination of these devices you can sleep at night content that your horses are not going to get out through the gates.

If I seem preoccupied with the problems of horses roaming through the suburban community, it's because I know of many horses who were killed or seriously injured while running loose. I've also known the wrath of horseless suburban neighbors when loose horses damaged their property.

♞ 8
Pasture and stable maintenance

Whether or not you succeed in recreating that dreamlike rural vista for your horse place, you will want to take care of your land and buildings to make the most of what you have. The way you maintain your stable and pasture will be important to your horse, your neighbors, and your family. You can go about it effectively and at the same time conserve your money and effort.

Practical pasture management

The saying "Fertilizer is cheaper than hay" may not always be true, but it suggests a useful management philosophy: It's better to encourage your own land to produce grass than to buy it from someone else. Fertilize your pasture heavily, close to the limit at which your soil will respond, to obtain maximum growth. Again, your great helper, the County Agricultural Agent, can tell you the kind of fertilizer, amount, and time of application that will be most effective in your locale.

You may have a neighbor with a mechanical spreader who will apply the fertilizer for you. If not, put it in a pail and spread it by walking back and forth and throwing it as you go, systematically covering the area. This is called "broadcasting." It will be easier, will provide uniform coverage, and will be good exercise.

Earlier I suggested that you keep horses out of the pasture when the ground is soft and muddy. This is essential if you want to grow grass. Also keep them out of the pasture in the spring until the new grass grows about 6 inches tall. Giving the grass this head start will greatly increase the amount of grass the horses get later, and it will help keep the weeds down.

If you can fence your pasture into two halves you can pasture half for a few days and then switch. This enables the grass to recover somewhat from being trampled on and overgrazed, and it should produce more.

Weed control in the pasture is both a problem and a necessity, especially in areas with ample rainfall for good plant growth. The weeds should be trimmed before the seeds form. The weeds probably will be concentrated in patches, and will grow more vigorously in the areas where the horses drop their manure. You can trim weeds with a scythe, but this is hard work and will consume a lot of your weekend horse-riding time. Perhaps a neighbor with a tractor and mower could clip your pasture a couple of times a summer.

Ideally, your pasture should be plowed and replanted every few years. This will help to keep a stand of the grasses you want and will keep the weeds under control. You can maintain desirable grasses if you sow grass seed annually on top of the ground to supplement the grass that is there. Late winter generally is a good time to sow the seed.

What to do in mud season

In parts of the country where the ground freezes in winter, the ground becomes very soft each time there is a thaw. In a February or March warm spell you can see horses standing knee deep in the mud of a small paddock. They are neither comfortable nor happy, for wet conditions often contribute to hoof problems. Horses can churn the whole area into a sea of mud. This destroys the turf, is unsightly, and greatly reduces the growth of grass later.

One way to prevent such damage is to keep the horses in their stalls during wet periods. Be sure to have maximum ventilation in the stalls, use plenty of bedding, and clean the stalls frequently. Another solution is to fence in a small enclosure by the stable and cover the ground with some material that will provide a firm base at all times. I've used stone dust about 6 inches deep, adding a little each year to maintain the base. The fence enclosing this small paddock should be a strong one.

Using stable space wisely

As I pointed out earlier, a horse does not need to be kept in a stall at all. A shed enclosed on three sides in which he can find protection from storms of winter and the hot sun of summer is enough. The open side of the shed should be away from the prevailing winter wind. If you keep him this way, he will be least likely to have winter colds.

You may prefer to use stalls rather than a shed, but remember, the more you keep the horse in the stall, the more work you will have. Your horse will be more contented and better off outside his stall most of the time if the stable has a roof overhang or some other protection against the elements. I usually keep my horses in stalls at night during winter weather and on days with severe winter storms, although if I had a shed they could go in and out as they please. I also let them in the stalls for brief periods to eat grain during the other seasons, when the pasture is poor, or when I can't get good hay. Some people keep their horses in stalls during the heat of the day in summer when flies are bad and turn them out to pasture at night, but I have plenty of shade, making this unnecessary.

A small stable with large box stalls and excellent ventilation. A floor with a rougher surface would be better, for smooth cement can be slippery.

Be sure to have very good ventilation in the stalls when the horses are in. If you have a small two- or three-stall barn, the air quickly becomes heavy with all the doors and windows closed and the stalls full of horses. I recommend installing Dutch doors and leaving the top half of each door open on all but the most stormy winter nights.

Controlling flies

Fly control requires more attention in the suburbs than on a farm because of the many neighbors who are likely to be bothered by flies and who may attribute the fly population to your horses, even though there may be another cause.

While you are consulting your County Agricultural Agent on other matters, obtain his advice on fly control. Climatic conditions vary so much that it is not possible to provide instructions that apply equally everywhere. Your County Agent can tell you about any local regulations and provide the latest scientific fly-control information for your area—which insecticides to use; how, when, and where to use them for greatest effectiveness and safety and in compliance with pesticide laws.

Flies will be attracted to your stable even if you keep it clean, but the cleaner it is, the fewer flies will congregate. You can hang old-fashioned flypaper in your feedroom and other places where horses and children will not get in it. You can buy electrical screens that are made as fly traps. Or you can use poison fly baits. Be careful to use poison only where horses, other animals, and children will have no opportunity to eat it. You also can spray with insecticide, being sure to use a product that will not endanger you or the horses.

I spray my stable frequently during the summer, using an insecticide formulated for the purpose and a small hand sprayer that makes a foglike mist. Electric foggers are sold especially for use in barns and stables, some automatically dispensing a fog of insecticide at predetermined intervals.

You may want to use fly repellent on your horses. This will be more for the health and enjoyment of the horse than for fly control in the community. Follow directions on the container. Repellent is usually applied sparingly around the eyes, mouth, and ears of the horse and near any cuts or sores.

Horses and manure attract several species of flies. The manure provides a place for them to multiply, particularly in warm and humid conditions. During the fly season, you should work a little harder than usual at cleaning stalls and disposing of manure.

Controlling rodents

Rodent control also demands your attention. You may not think there are mice and rats in your community, but once you build a stable and have a supply of feed constantly available, they will appear. And there may be more of them than the family cat can handle.

You may be willing to accept a few mice, but you don't want any rats in your stable. You also don't want the neighbors to think that you are supporting a reservoir of rats to visit and migrate to their places. Both rats and mice, in addition to the damage they can cause to the stable itself, may destroy valuable tack and will eat a large amount of horse feed—if you let them.

You can reduce the problem by keeping grain in a mouse-proof container—a tight feedbox, metal garbage can, or other closed container. Manure contains some undigested grain, providing some feed for rodents no matter how careful you are. Cleanliness, in addition to its virtue, is important for rodent control. Muck out the stalls often, and dispose of all empty feedbags immediately.

If you catch each rat as soon as it arrives, before it can be joined by others and raise a family, control will be easiest. In my tack room I placed a small box with a hole in one side large enough to admit a rat. I keep a small amount of rat poison in it, just waiting for any passing rodents that may consider making my stable their home. Most rat poisons contain Warfarin, a chemical that thins the blood and prohibits coagulation. It affects all animals, so be careful where you put it—away from horses, dogs, and children.

What to do with all that manure

Disposing of manure and soiled bedding is a necessary chore that need not be time-consuming. What's more, the manure can be turned into a valuable asset, thus converting a problem into an opportunity.

Some horses will save you work by placing most of their manure outside the shed or in one corner of the shed or stall. (There probably is some way to train a horse to do this, but I'm not acquainted with it.)

If you have a shed for shelter, keep the shed floor covered with plenty of straw, shavings, or other bedding. Then you will have to clean it out only occasionally, depending on the number of horses using the shed, how well the floor drains, the weather, and perhaps the nearness of your neighbors. Back home on the farm when I was growing up, we let manure pile up all winter in the stalls on the theory that the decaying organic material created a heat that helped to keep the horses warm on cold winter nights—a practice not recommended for parasite control and certainly not good in a suburban community.

If you keep your horses in stalls except when they're being exercised, you should use plenty of bedding and clean out the manure and soiled bedding daily. That alone is a good reason to have enough land so you won't have to keep them in stalls.

The amount of space you have and the way you manage your horses will determine the amount of time you spend handling and disposing of manure. Using my summer system of putting the horses in the stalls only for feeding grain, the stalls need cleaning only once every three or four weeks in the summer. With the winter system—keeping horses in the stalls at night and having a deep layer of bedding—the stalls usually need cleaning weekly. If you keep horses in stalls during hot summer days, you probably will have to clean daily because of the greater fly and odor problems at that time.

You need a compost pit

A facility you may find almost essential is a compost pit or pile where manure and other organic wastes can decay. It should be more than a stack in the backyard for all the community to see and smell.

You can go about it as organic gardeners do. Build a rectangular enclosure of boards, cement blocks, or other material. Dig a pit on a slope so it will not fill with water during wet periods, or build your compost pile directly on the ground. You can screen it from view with a few well-placed shrubs. Decay will be rapid because of the high quantity of nitrogen available and because of the heat that is created. Adding lime to the pile will help to control odors. If you are a gardener, use the well-decayed compost liberally in your garden. You can mix in great quantities without harm or use it as a mulch on top of the soil. Soon your flowers and vegetables will be the envy of the community. You will be the person with the green thumb.

If you still have enough of this excellent organic matter, let your gardening neighbors in on the secret. Offer decayed organic matter to all of your neighbors who garden but do not have horses. There is nothing wrong with the sub-soil builders may have left around the house that nature will not take care of with plenty of rotted organic matter. When their flowers and vegetables prosper they will be grateful—and much more tolerant of horses in the community. This is the modern way of natural recycling, and it is a great way to make friends.

Another practice I have found useful is to accumulate manure in the compost pile until late winter. When the heat of the pile has killed most of the parasite eggs and weed seeds and the manure is fairly well decayed, spread it in a thin and uniform layer in the areas of the pasture most heavily grazed the previous year. Then sow grass seed on these areas. The manure helps the old and new grass to start growing vigorously, and it encourages the horses to graze in other spots for a while when they are turned out in spring.

In the pasture your horses probably will concentrate their manure in certain areas and let the grass grow long there—nature's defense against parasites. If you break up the piles the elements will help kill parasite eggs and birds and rain will disperse the manure more quickly.

Some people recommend that you go around the pasture with a pitchfork and wheelbarrow, hauling away all the manure on the ground. This may be necessary in small paddocks in arid areas, but it is a lot of work. My experience is that it's unnecessary in a climate with frequent rains and some birds to help you.

The easy way to spread piles of manure is to go over your pasture with a "drag" pulled behind a small tractor. You can do this on half your pasture after you have moved the horses to the other half, so the natural elements can work on the manure before the horses return to graze.

♞ 9
The horseman and the community

You and your family are certain to get much more enjoyment and satisfaction from owning a horse if you have community approval. A community that accepts horses and provides for them is invariably a community in which there are more opportunities to enjoy using the horse and more people who share your hobby. Horsemen can work together to develop community acceptance and support. Horsemen can also cooperate in providing some of their common needs—riding facilities, horse health services, feed and other supplies, and horse activities.

How do horsemen work together to increase their enjoyment from owning and using horses? Among the many needs and organizations in your area, you are sure to find opportunities to use your particular talents effectively in ways that will be helpful to you, to other horsemen, and to your community.

Community events

Competitions and shows

Many horsemen, particularly young people, enjoy and benefit from shows, rodeos, and other contests or events in which

Local horse clubs offer invaluable assistance to novice riders. Here, a pony-club instructor prepares an attentive class for a jumping lesson.

they display their skills and their horses. A community show or contest adds excitement to the horse hobby and provides a goal toward which to work. Fast friendships are often developed and, perhaps most important, the participants win recognition for their accomplishments.

No show or contest succeeds without a lot of people working together, planning and doing the many jobs that must be done. No horse event can be conducted without a riding ring or some other facility, which must be maintained, prepared for the show, and cleaned up afterward. The whole thing requires an organized group of people working together to create a successful and enjoyable event. In your community there probably already is an organization of people who help put on horse events. Your talents will be welcome.

Local horse clubs

Many communities have horse clubs for adults and youth that provide a variety of services decided upon by the members. Some sponsor horse shows and trail-rides; some maintain trail systems, riding rings, or other facilities. Frequently they speak on behalf of horsemen to local zoning boards and park authorities. Some sponsor educational activities, including training clinics and management schools. Others contribute to scientific research in horse nutrition and management. If you look around, you probably will find such an organization in your area. If not, you can join with some neighbors and organize one.

One or more organizations in your area may serve people who are interested in a particular horse activity, such as a hunt club, dressage club, a large show, or a rodeo. Joining such an organization can expand your own interests and skills.

Youth programs

Young horsemen want to learn more about horses and their care. They want to develop their horse-related knowledge and skills. And they enjoy doing these things while associating with their friends.

Most communities have 4-H horse clubs, pony clubs, and other horse organizations for youth. These groups are largely educational, but they serve social needs as well. They sponsor shows and other contests and demonstrations; they also provide opportunities to participate in regional, state, and national events that provide broad educational experiences and greater opportunities for achievement and recognition.

At the end of 1974, 320,767 4-H members were involved in horse projects. The 4-H clubs are supervised by your County Agricultural Agent. He or she should be able to tell you about other horse organizations for youth and adults serving these needs. These clubs need adult leaders to help organize activities, act as instructors, and pass on to young people some of their knowledge and skill.

Adults who are new to horse ownership need new knowledge and skills too. They can learn by working with the more experienced horsemen in the community.

Cooperative action

By using the time-tested principles of farmers' cooperatives, horsemen can work together to buy feed, supplies, and fertilizer at lower cost in large quantities. Through cooperatives they also can buy services—fence building, fertilizer spreading, mowing, and others. They may own an arena or stable for their joint use. The prevention and control of horse diseases, a concern of all horsemen, is accomplished best by group action. Cooperative members can bring their horses to a central location, where a veterinarian can easily vaccinate or treat a number of horses in a short time.

Programs of quarantine, vaccination, and disease eradication are administered by a variety of state and federal agencies. Interest in and support of these programs by horsemen's organizations is vital to their success. Support, vigilance, and interest are also important to many other government actions that involve horsemen—such as land-use laws, programs to prevent cruelty to animals, and many more.

Community relations

The great non-horse majority of people in your community, if not well informed about good management on limited acreage, may take public action that restricts opportunities for horsemen to pursue and enjoy their hobby. Restrictions may include health regulations, building codes, conservation and land-use rules, and a variety of other regulations. But if horsemen work together to see that others are adequately informed, the majority may take public action that enhances and expands opportunities for enjoying horses to benefit the whole community—providing equestrian trails, show rings, and permissive zoning.

As pressures on our limited supply of land increase with expanding population, the amount of land-use regulation also increases. When areas once rural are developed rapidly for suburban housing, many suburban and nearby rural areas pass zoning or other ordinances restricting one's ability to keep a horse and regulating conditions under which horses are kept. In some cases these have been developed with help of horsemen; in other cases they have been developed with little knowledge of horses or horsemen and their needs and include unnecessarily restrictive provisions.

Some amount of regulation of this sort is certainly desirable and necessary. For example, if one were to keep several horses in a stable on a half-acre lot in a community of half-acre lots, it would be almost impossible to avoid creating a nuisance.

Taking a horse over a barrel jump at a local horse-club meeting.

The big question is not whether the majority in a suburban community is going to regulate the keeping of horses by a small minority. The major questions are if horses will be permitted at all, and under what specific conditions. All people in a community have a stake in the answers to these questions. And the answers depend to a large extent on the horsemen now there—on the facilities they have, on the way they manage their land and horses, and on the interest they take in helping develop regulations that serve and protect the interests of horsemen and non-horsemen alike.

My personal experience as a suburban horseman is in Fairfax County, Virginia, a suburb of Washington, D.C. There, county zoning requires at least a 2-acre lot to keep a horse and specifies that a stable be at least 40 feet from lot lines. No limitation has been placed on the number of horses one can keep on the 2 acres, nor do the ordinances specify management practices. Recently there has been public discussion of more restrictive regulations. If I lived next door to some of the 2-acre horse places I have seen, I might be joining such a cause myself.

Land developers, government administrators, and individual citizens are much more likely to favor continued and expanded use of horses if horses in the area are well cared for and if organized horsemen have worked together to make their needs and interests known.

Special land developments for horse lovers

Zoning sometimes provides areas where lots must be 2, 3, 5, or 10 acres in size. Such areas frequently are designated specifically to appeal to people with horses. Developers of such tracts may include easements for riding trails adjacent to each lot or set aside land for a community riding ring or stable. Sometimes protective covenants limit the number of horses that can be kept and restrict the design and location of stables and types of fences to protect the interests of the community.

A Boston mortgage insurance company predicts that the horse–ranch house (an oversized lot including landscaped paddock and stable areas) will become more and more popular in suburban areas across the country, reflecting the increased popularity of horses and people's concern for physical fitness.

Trail-riding

Many suburban horsemen, young and old alike, enjoy trail-riding—alone and at their own pace, or in groups, perhaps combined with picnicking, camping, or competitive endurance rides. Obviously, for trail-riding there have to be trails on someone's land, public or private. Someone must build these trails, maintain them, and provide some policing. Here, in our rapidly urbanizing society, lie some special opportunities for horsemen.

Riding trails are more readily available in some suburban areas than in some very rural areas, mainly because people interested in horse activities have provided them. In recent years, the public has greatly expanded its interest in all kinds of outdoor recreation. If incomes, population, and the amount of leisure time continue to increase, this trend seems certain to continue.

Currently, a national movement to provide a network of recreational trails for equestrians, pedestrians, and cyclists is gaining momentum. Horsemen involved in this movement visualize the day when we can ride our horses from border to border and coast to coast on this trail system. An important start has been made toward developing such a system.

In many urban and suburban areas, groups are working with park authorities and other local units of government to develop local trail systems, which may eventually be linked together into state and national systems. Limited federal money is provided to help in these local developments; federal and state funds may also be available to help develop other facilities of interest to horesemen, such as loading ramps, camping facilities, and show rings.

Horsemen, working individually and through a variety of organizations, can help the trail system grow so that the trails serve their needs. In fact, unless horsemen participate and let their needs be known, some trails may exclude horses.

National and state parks and forests are ideal places for trail-riding. One or more is within horse-trailer distance of most horsemen. Some public parks and forests have extensive systems of excellent bridle trails (see Appendix). On the other hand, some that are conveniently located for large numbers of suburban horsemen have none, or even prohibit horseback riding.

Experiences of several horsemen's organizations in recent years tell us that many of the agencies and people managing public lands are receptive to providing riding trails and related facilities. Organized horsemen should express the need effectively and offer their help in building and maintaining these facilities. Closer to home, many opportunities for expanding recreational trails for use by horsemen, hikers, and others exist in or near almost every suburban community.

Horsemen's organizations

Individual horsemen, working alone, can help serve some of the needs of the community of horsemen. But their effectiveness and accomplishments are multiplied when they work together. Most suburban communities have a number of horse-related organizations, many of which are affiliated with state and national groups.

A host of organizations promotes the ownership, use, and enjoyment of particular breeds of horses. Two local examples are the Blue Ridge Arabian Horse Association and the Virginia Quarter Horse Association. Many of these organizations con-

Many communities, such as this one in Kentucky, are establishing bridle trails on public lands to serve the growing numbers of pleasure-horse owners.

duct horse shows, sales, and other activities of interest to breeders and owners of horses of that breed. Typically they also participate in activities of interest to horsemen in general, contribute to research, and act as lobbyists for the horse industry. Some have junior affiliates for promoting youth activities using horses of that breed. In the Appendix is a list of national breed organizations. Write to them to learn about state and regional organizations for those breeds.

State horse councils have been organized in most states. They serve as a vital communications link among horse groups within the state and help to coordinate many horse-related organizations. They can be very effective in speaking for horsemen and expressing their interests and needs to state legislators, agencies of government, members of Congress, and the general public. Some also conduct statewide horse activities. State horse councils are listed in the Appendix.

The American Horse Council serves a similar need on the national scene. The Council, formed and supported by a large number of national, regional, and special horse-related organizations, provides a vital communications link between all parts of the horse industry and the several branches of the federal government. The organization has an important influence on research to benefit horsemen, programs aimed at controlling animal diseases, use of horses on federal land, recreation planning, and a variety of other regulations affecting horsemen.

These are only a few of the organizations that relate the horsemen to the community. There are, of course, many groups that are oriented toward recreation, natural resources, conservation, agriculture, and local fairs.

♞ 10

How to find out more

Other sources of information

This book has not discussed learning to ride, breeding horses, nor participating in special horse events. These are subjects that are treated in specialized books.

Some readers may want more detail on some of the subjects we have discussed. To help you find added information I have included in the Appendix a list of books that are considered good sources. Of course this is only a small fraction of the good books available.

Magazines for horsemen are another excellent source of information. They include listings of shows, sales, sources of supplies and equipment, and articles by horsemen on a variety of subjects. You may want to subscribe to one or more, so I have listed some of the national publications. Others that are directed at a state or regional audience are not included.

The United States Department of Agriculture is an excellent source of reliable (and often free) information on a variety of subjects related to agriculture. In the list of books are several USDA publications of interest to horse people. You should be able to obtain these from your County Extension Service office (there is one in nearly every county—check the telephone book under the county's name), from the Government Printing

Office (write to the Superintendent of Documents, U.S. Government Printing Office, Washington, D.C. 20402), or by writing to the U.S. Department of Agriculture, Washington, D.C. 20250.

At several points I have recommended your County Agricultural Agent as a source of scientific information. He or she is in your County Extension Service office and is employed cooperatively by your state land-grant college and the USDA.

Most land-grant universities have a horse specialist who works with County Agents and the people they serve, providing the latest scientific information. A list of these Extension horse specialists is in the Appendix. Each land-grant university also has special publications it has developed for horsemen. Get a list from your County Agent.

There are many other public servants employed to help you as horsemen in a variety of ways. Your land-grant college has an Agricultural Experiment Station that conducts research on agricultural problems, including horse health. The Animal and Plant Health Inspection Service of the USDA has a number of programs to eradicate or control certain animal diseases and pests. For example, this agency chased Venezuelan encephalitis back across the Mexican border. Each state government has a unit devoted to administering state laws related to animal health. Some of these units provide blood tests and other laboratory services for horsemen.

Many of the lists in the Appendix are provided by the American Horse Council in their publication, *Horse Industry Trade Press Directory*. The Council plans to revise and update the directory annually.

A final note on safety

The horse hobby really isn't dangerous. Don't be afraid of it, or of horses. But a horse is a big and heavy animal. If he steps on your foot you will know it. One kick can kill. Falling off can break bones, or worse. It pays to be cautious: so know the safety rules, and make the practice of them routine.

There is a small USDA publication that gives you all the safety rules you need. Call your County Agent today and ask him to send you *Horse Safety Guidelines.*

The keynote is enjoyment

Throughout the book I have discussed alternate ways of doing things, and various costs. One of my goals has been to help you decide whether to get a horse, if the decision was not already made. You may have decided not to own a horse.

You can enjoy horses without owning them. Learn to ride. There are plenty of places where you can rent a horse by the hour. There are many people whose horses do not have enough exercise and who would be delighted to let a good rider ride free.

In spring drive out to a nearby horse farm and watch the mares and their foals play in the pasture. There is no creature so lovable as a newborn, long-legged, clumsy foal, nor a mother more loving, tolerant, and protective than an old mare.

Go to local horse shows and help do the jobs that make the shows run smoothly. Or go to the races and visit the paddock to see the jockeys saddle up. Walk by the barns and sense the excitement—and the relaxation when the race is done.

Stop any time along a pasture fence and admire the beauty and grace of young horses galloping freely in the pasture.

Or come out to my place and sit with me with our feet on the porch rail watching the horses enjoy the cool of the evening.

Appendix

Glossary

Aids—a system of signals by which the rider communicates instructions to the horse through hands, legs, feet, and voice.

A-I—artificial insemination, a technique of breeding animals without natural union.

Alfalfa—a leguminous plant used for feed, high in protein. Also called "lucerne."

American Saddle Horse—a recognized breed that combines Thoroughbred and native lines.

Appaloosa—a horse breed developed by an Indian tribe in the Northwest; characterized by unique spotted markings.

Arab, Arabian—a horse breed that originated in the Arabian desert; characterized by endurance and speed.

Bay—a horse color—the coat is dark brown; tail, mane, and legs are black.

Bedding—straw, shavings, or other inedible materials used to cushion the floor of a stall.

Blaze—a marked area of white color on the face of a horse extending from forehead to nostrils.

Bloodline—the ancestry of a horse.

Bloodworm—an internal parasite.

Bog spavin—an unsoundness of the leg in which the hock swells.

Bots—an internal parasite.

Box stall—an area in a stable for keeping a horse, usually large enough so the horse can turn around.

Broodmare—a female horse used for breeding.

Break—a word meaning "to train" or "to gentle."

Buckskin—a horse color—yellowish body with black mane and tail; also used interchangeably with "dun."

Cannon—the bones below the knee and above the fetlock in a horse's front and hind legs.

Canter—a three-beat gait; known in Western riding as a "lope."

Chestnut—a horse color—usually solid reddish brown on body, mane, and tail.

Class—an event at a horse show.

Colostrum—the first milk produced by an animal after giving birth.

Colt—a male horse not over three years old.

Creep—a pen where a foal can be fed grain but the mother cannot enter.

Cribbing—a bad habit or vice in which the horse bites a fixed object, pulls back with the head, and sucks in air.

Crossbred—a horse of mixed breeding, usually used to designate a horse with one Thoroughbred parent.

Croup—the line of the back of the horse just forward of the tail.

Curb—a type of bit that exerts considerable leverage on the horse's mouth.

Curry comb—a blunt-toothed comb used in grooming a horse to scrape away loose hair and dirt.

Dam—a foal's mother.

Draft horses—breeds adapted for pulling heavy loads.

Dressage—a programmed riding test involving various gaits and maneuvers.

Dun—a horse color—ranging from yellowish-brown to bluish-gray, sometimes with a dark stripe down the spine (see "buckskin").

E.I.A.—equine infectious anemia, or swamp fever.

Equestrian—having to do with horses; also, a person who rides horses.

Equine, equus—technical term for the horse species.

Estrus—a recurrent state in the female reproductive cycle (estrous cycle), during which the animal will accept breeding.

Farrier—one who cares for the feet of horses, including shoeing.

Fertilization—the joining of sperm and egg in the breeding process; also, the application of chemicals to the soil.

Filly—a female horse not over three years old.

Floating—a process of removing rough spots on the horse's teeth.

Foal—a young or newly-born horse of either sex, under a year in age.

Forequarter—the front half of the horse.

Founder—an inflammation of the hoof, also called "laminitis."

Frog—the triangular-shaped area in the center of the bottom of the hoof.

Gaits—the several ways a horse can travel; usually includes walk, trot, canter, and gallop.

Gallop—a rapid, four-beat gait; the fastest way of traveling.

Gelding—a male that has been castrated.

Grade—a horse that is not registered in any breed registry.

Hand—a unit of measure used to designate height of horses at the withers; one hand is four inches.

Heat period—the part of the estrous cycle during which the mare will accept breeding; also called estrus.

Heaves—a serious respiratory disease.

Hock—the joint that is halfway down the rear leg.

Hunter—a type of horse used for fox hunting; not a breed.

Interfering—the condition in which one hoof strikes the opposite leg when the horse moves.

Longe—to make a horse travel in a circle on the end of a rope while the trainer stands in the center.

Mare—a mature female horse, over three years old.

Morgan—a breed developed in New England; characterized by its versatility and strength.

Pace—any one of the gaits of a horse; also used to describe a harness-horse gait in which both feet on one side leave the ground together, as opposed to the "trot."

Palomino—a horse color—tan or gold with white mane and tail; also, generally recognized as a breed.

Pastern—the short bones just above a horse's hoofs.

Pedigree—the ancestry of an animal.

Pinto—a horse color—large areas of brown or black on white; in America, recognized as a breed.

Poll—the area between a horse's ears.

Put down—to destroy a horse humanely.

Quarter Horse—a breed characterized by agility and the ability to run short distances at high speed.

Roan—a horse color—colored hairs (black, red, gray, or brown) with a large number of white hairs mixed in.

Roughage—the hay and grass in the horse ration.

Shipping fever—a common respiratory disease or group of diseases.

Snip—a small white marking on the nose.

Sock—a white marking on the legs as far up as the fetlock.

Smooth-mouthed—teeth so worn down that it is difficult to tell age, usually occurring at about nine years.

Splint—a bony growth in the lower leg, often causing lameness.

Standardbred—a breed of horse used mostly for harness racing.

Star—a small spot of white color on the forehead.

Stocking—a white marking on the legs as far as the knee or hock; higher than socks.

Straw—the stalks of a grain plant, harvested for use as bedding.

Stud—a stallion or male horse.

Swamp fever—equine infectious anemia.

Tack—saddles, bridles, halters, grooming tools, and similar equipment.

Thoroughbred—a breed of horse developed primarily for racing.

Thrush—a decay of the hoof caused by standing in a wet, dirty stall.

Trot—a two-beat, diagonal gait.

Unsoundness—a defect sufficiently serious to impair the health or use of a horse.

V.E.E.—Venezuelan equine encephalitis, a form of sleeping sickness.

Weaving—the shifting of weight from side to side while a horse stands.

Withers—the part of the horse's back just above the shoulders.

Yearling—a horse of either sex that is one year old but not yet two.

Bibliography

American Quarter Horse Association, *Nutrient Requirements of the Light Horse.* P.O. Box 200, Amarillo, Texas 79168. A technical publication with detailed information about horse nutrition.

——*Training Riding Horses.* A small pamphlet providing tips on training from successful and well-known trainers.

Davidson, Joseph B., D.V.M. *Horseman's Veterinary Adviser.* New York, Arco, 1973. Discusses several hundred illnesses and health problems in layman's language.

Ensminger, M.E., *Horses and Horsemanship.* Interstate Printers and Publishers, Inc., Danville, Illinois 61832, 1969. An authority covers a wide range of technical matters involved in selection, care, feeding, health, and other subjects.

Evans, Edna H., *Famous Horses and Their People.* Brattleboro, Vermont, The Stephen Greene Press, 1975. Fascinating tales of famous people and the horses linked to their lives.

Forbes, Joanne. *So Your Kids Want a Pony!* Brattleboro, Vermont, The Stephen Greene Press, 1972. Guidance for the family contemplating buying a pony, including selection, care, and activities.

Goodall, Daphne Machin, *Horses of the World.* New York, The MacMillan Company, 1965. Provides information about the many breeds of horses.

International Arabian Horse Association, *The Golden Book of Arabian Horse Showing.* 224 East Olive Avenue, Burbank, California 91502. Detailed information about horse showing, judging, and show management, written for Arabian owners but applicable to other breeds.

Kays, John M., *The Horse.* New York, Arco, 1969. An authoritative book covering the judging, breeding, feeding, management, and selling of horses.

Kenoyer, Natlee. *Gymkhana Games.* Brattleboro, Vermont, The Stephen Greene Press, 1972. Describes more than fifty games and timed events for people on horseback.

Lungwitz, A., translated by John W. Adams, *Textbook of Horseshoeing.* Corvallis, Oregon, Oregon State University Press, 1966. A reprint of a classic reputed to be one of the best manuals on the subject ever published. First published in German in 1884.

Midwest Plan Service, *Horse Handbook, Housing and Equipment.* Ames, Iowa, Iowa State University Press. Contains information about different types of horse barns and their construction; lists available plans.

Podhajsky, Alois, *The Complete Training of Horse and Rider.* Garden City, New York, Doubleday & Company, 1967. An internationally recognized expert gives detailed instructions on training the horse and rider, starting at the beginning and progressing through dressage.

Price, Steven D., *Horseback Vacation Guide*. Brattleboro, Vermont, The Stephen Greene Press, 1975. A specific and practical guide to horseback vacation opportunities in the United States, Canada, and elsewhere.

Smythe, R.H., *The Mind of the Horse*. Brattleboro, Vermont, The Stephen Greene Press, 1965. Covers horse vision, hearing, senses of smell and taste, emotions, and psychology.

Straiton, E.C., *The Horse Owner's Vet Book*. New York, J.B. Lippincott Company, 1973. A readable source of information about the many diseases, illnesses, and unsoundnesses of horses.

United States Department of Agriculture, Agricultural Handbook No. 394, *Breeding and Raising Horses*. Washington, D.C., U.S. Government Printing Office. A reliable source of information on many aspects of breeding and raising horses. Available through County Agents' offices at low cost.

————Farmers Bulletin No. 2247, *Fences for the Farm and Rural Home*. Describes advantages and disadvantages of different types of fencing materials and fences. Available through County Agents' offices.

————Agricultural Information Bulletin No. 353, *Horsemanship and Horse Care*. Information on horse nutrition, diseases, parasites, riding, and other subjects. Available through County Agents' offices.

————Extension Service Bulletin, *Horse Safety Guidelines*. Covers all aspects of safety in keeping and riding horses. Available through County Agents' offices.

————Agricultural Handbook No. 438, *Recreation Buildings and Facilities*. Contains sketches of easy-to-build recreational facilities, including horse stalls of various sizes and designs. Detailed building plans are also offered. Available through County Agents' offices.

State horse councils

Alaska State Horsemen, Inc.
2422 Telequana Dr.
Anchorage, AK 99503

California Horse Council
224 E. Olive Ave., Suite 305
Burbank, CA 91502

Colorado Horsemen's Council
P.O. Box 493
Golden, CO 80401

Connecticut Horse Council
73 Cutler Rd.
Greenwich, CT 06830

Florida Horse Council
1800 SW 3rd. St.
Pompano Beach, FL 33060

Idaho Horse Council
c/o Ed Duren
P.O. Box 29
Soda Springs, ID 83276

Kentucky Horse Council
P.O. Box 11992
Lexington, KY 40511

Massachusetts Horsemen's Council
117 Grove St.
Upton, MA 01568

Michigan Horse Council
P.O. Box 494
Lansing, MI 48902

Minnesota Horse Council
P.O. Box 292
Long Lake, MN 55356

Mississippi Horse Council
700 Main St.
Columbia, MS 39429

Missouri Horse & Mule Council
Box 101
Lynn Creek, MO 65052

New Jersey Horse Council
310 West State St.
Trenton, NJ 08618

New Mexico Horse Council
P.O. Box 10206
Alameda, NM 87114

New York Horse Council
P.O. Box 187
Purchase, NY 10577

North Carolina Horse Council
P.O. Box 25871
Raleigh, NC 27611

Ohio Horseman's Council
P.O. Box 244
Miami Town, OH 45041

Oklahoma Horsemen's Association
2525 Northwest Expressway
Oklahoma City, OK 73112

Oregon Horsemen's Association
3835 River Rd.
Eugene, OR 97404

Pennsylvania Equine Council
324 Animal Industry Bldg.
University Park, PA 16802

South Carolina Horse Council
c/o Larry Hudson
Extension Horse Specialist
Clemson University
Clemson, SC 29631

South Dakota Horse Council
c/o Josephine Waldner
P.O. Box 272
Brookings, SD 57006

Texas Horse Council
c/o Tex Rogers
5314 Bingle Road
Houston, TX 77018

Vermont Horsemen's Council
RFD #1, Box 1LA
Ludlow, VT 05149

Virginia Horse Council
P.O. Box 72
Riner, VA 24149

Washington State Horsemen, Inc.
P.O. Box X
Kirkland, WA 98033

West Virginia Horse Council
c/o David Keith
West Virginia Department of
  Agriculture
Charleston, WV 25305

Wisconsin State Horse Council
1675 Observatory Dr.
Madison, WI 53706

Horsemen's organizations

General

The American Horse Council
1700 K St., N.W.
Washington, D.C. 20006

Equestrian

American Horse Shows Association
527 Madison Ave.
New York, NY 10022

American Vaulting Association
P.O. Box 1307
San Juan Bautista, CA 95045

International Side-Saddle
Association
R.D. 2, Box 2096
Mount Holly, NJ 08060

National Steeplechase and Hunt
Association
P.O. Box 308
Elmont, NY 11003

U.S. Combined Training Association
One Winthrop Square
Boston, MA 02110

U.S. Dressage Federation
c/o Lowell Boomer
Box 80668
Lincoln, NB 68501

U.S. Polo Association
1301 W. 22nd St., Suite 706
Oak Brook, IL 60521

Handicapped

National Foundation for Happy
Horsemanship for the
Handicapped
Box 462
Malvern, PA 19355

North American Riding for the
Handicapped
c/o Cheff Center for the
Handicapped
Box 171
Augusta, MI 49012

Youth

Future Farmers of America
P.O. Box 15160
Alexandria, VA 22309

National 4-H Service Committee
150 N. Wacker Dr.
Chicago, IL 60606

National Horse and Pony Youth
Activities Council
c/o Jack Huyler, President
Thacher School
Ojai, CA 93023

U.S. Pony Clubs
303 S. High St.
West Chester, PA 19380

State extension specialists in animal science

Note: Full-time horse specialists are marked with an asterisk. All Extension Specialists are well qualified and will provide leadership for horse programs.

Bob Whittenburg
Auburn University
Auburn, AL 36830

Albert M. Lane
University of Arizona
P.O. Box 790
Tucson, AZ 85721

Robert C. McDaniel
University of Arkansas
P.O. Box 391
Little Rock, AR 72203

*Reuben Albaugh
University of California
Davis, CA 95616

*William Culbertson
Colorado State University
Fort Collins, CO 80521

*Robert C. Church
University of Connecticut
Storrs, CT 06268

*C. Melvin Reitnour
University of Delaware
Newark, DE 19711

*Ben Crawford
University of Florida
Gainesville, FL 32601

*Charles A. Hutton
University of Georgia
Coliseum
Athens, GA 30602

Harry R. Donoho
University of Hawaii
P.O. Box 237
Kamuela, HI 96743

Edward P. Duren
University of Idaho
P.O. Box 638
Soda Springs, ID 83276

*Mark A. Russell
Dept. of Animal Science
University of Illinois
Urbana, IL 61801

*R. A. Battaglia
2-112 Lilly
Purdue University
Lafayette, IN 47907

Tom Wickersham
Iowa State University
Ames, IA 50010

Wendell A. Moyer
Kansas State University
Manhattan, KS 66505

*Steve Jackson
University of Kentucky
Lexington, KY 40506

*Calvin O. McKerley
Louisiana State University
Baton Rouge, LA 70803

*John C. Goater, Jr.
University of Maine
Orono, ME 04473

*Edwin E. Goodwin
University of Maryland
College Park, MD 20742

Carol Collyer
University of Massachusetts
Amherst, MA 01002

*Richard J. Dunn
Michigan State University
East Lansing, MI 48824

*Robert M. Jordan
University of Minnesota
St. Paul, MN 55101

Duane H. Tucker
Mississippi State University
State College, MS 39762

*Melvin Bradley
University of Missouri
Columbia, MO 65201

Roger M. Brownson
Montana State University
Bozeman, MT 59715

Richard B. Warren
University of Nebraska
Lincoln, NE 68503

*Douglas A. Reynolds
University of Nevada
Reno, NV 89507

Susan Kelleher
University of New Hampshire
Kendall Hall
Durham, NH 03824

*O. Frederick Harper
Rutgers - The State University
Box 231
New Brunswick, NJ 08903

W.J. Ljungdahl
New Mexico State University
Drawer AE
Las Cruces, NM 88001

*Samuel W. Sabin
Cornell University
Ithaca, NY 14850

*Tom Leonard
North Carolina State University
Raleigh, NC 27607

Wallace Eide
Animal Extension Specialist
North Dakota State University
Fargo, ND 58102

*Robert C. Kline
Ohio State University
2029 Fyffe Rd.
Columbus, OH 43210

Joe Hughes
Oklahoma State University
Stillwater, OK 74074

Dean Frischknecht
Oregon State University
212 Withycombe
Corvallis, OR 97331

*J.P. Gallagher
Pennsylvania State University
University Park, PA 16802

Carlos Gaztambide-Arrillaga
University of Puerto Rico
Box AR
Rio Piedras, PR 00927

B. Henderson
University of Rhode Island
Kingston, RI 02881

*L. W. Hudson
Clemson University
Clemson, SC 29631

Francis Crandall
South Dakota State University
West River Agriculture Research
   and Extension Center
801 E. San Francisco
Rapid City, SD 57701

Haley M. Jamison
University of Tennessee
P.O. Box 1071
Knoxville, TN 37901

*B. F. Yeates
Texas A & M University
College Station, TX 77843

*Don W. Thomas
Utah State University
Logan, UT 84321

D.J. Balch
Animal Science Dept.
University of Vermont
Burlington, VT 05401

*Arden N. Huff
Virginia Polytechnic Institute
Blacksburg, VA 24061

Joe B. Johnson
Washington State University
Pullman, WA 99163

B. W. Wamsley, Jr.
West Virginia University
Morgantown, WV 26506

*Ray Antoniewicz
University of Wisconsin
Madison, WI 53706

Oliver Hall
University of Wyoming
Box 3354
Laramie, WY 82071

Magazines for horsemen

American Horseman
257 Park Ave. South
New York, NY 10010
(general interest)

American Shetland Pony Journal
P.O. Box 468
Fowler, IN 47944
(breed)

Appaloosa News
P.O. Box 8403
Moscow, ID 83843
(breed)

The Appy
15039 Rock Creek Rd.
Charden, OH 44024
(breed)

The Arabian Horse
1777 Wynkoop St., Rm. 1
Denver, CO 80202
(breed)

The Arabian Horse News
P.O. Box 2264
Ft. Collins, CO 80522
(breed)

Arabian Horse World
815 San Antonio Rd.
Palo Alto, CA 94303
(breed)

Carriage Journal
RD #1, Box 115
Salem, NJ 08079
(carriages and carts)

Chronicle of the Horse
Middleburg, VA 22117
(Thoroughbred in sport)

Cuttin' Hoss Chatter
P.O. Box 12155
Fort Worth, TX 76116
(show)

Draft Horse Journal
Rt. 3
Waverly, IA 50677
(breed)

Dressage
P.O. Box 2460
Cleveland, OH 44112
(show)

Equestrian Trails
P.O. Box 2086
North Hollywood, CA 91602
(trails)

The Hackney Journal
P.O. Box 630
Peekskill, NY 10566
(breed)

Hoof & Horn
P.O. Box C
Englewood, CO 80110
(rodeo)

Horse & Horseman
P.O. Box HH
Capistrano Beach, CA 92624
(general interest)

Horse and Rider
Box 555
Temecula, CA 92390
(general interest)

Horse Lover's National Magazine
651 Brannan St.
San Francisco, CA 94107
(general interest)

Horseman
5314 Bingle Rd.
Houston, TX 77018
(general interest)

Horse, Of Course!
Derbyshire Bldg.
Temple, NH 03084
(general interest)

Horse Play
50-B Ridge Rd.
Greenbelt, MD 20770
(youth)

Horse Show
527 Madison Ave.
New York, NY 10022
(show)

The Horsetrader, Inc.
4131 Erie St.
Willoughby, OH 44094
(sales and ads)

Horse World
P.O. Box 588
Lexington, KY 40501
(show)

The Lariat
12675 S.W. 1st St.
Beaverton, OR 97005
(general interest)

The Morgan Horse
P.O. Box 29, West Lake Moraine
   Rd.
Hamilton, NY 13346
(breed)

The National Horseman
P.O. Box 4067, Baxter Station
Louisville, KY 40204
(show)

The Paint Horse Journal
P.O. Box 13486
Fort Worth, TX 76118
(breed)

Palomino Horses
P.O. Box 249
Mineral Wells, TX 76067
(breed)

Peruvian Horse Review
P.O. Box 816
Guerneville, CA 95446
(breed)

Peruvian Horse World
P.O. Box 2035
California City, CA 93505
(breed)

The Pinto Horse
P.O. Box 3984
San Diego, CA 92103
(breed)

Polo News
P.O. Box 855
Middleburg, VA 22117
(polo)

Pony of the Americas
P.O. Box 1447
Mason City, IA 50401
(breed)

Quarter Horse Digest
Gann Valley, SD 57341
(breed)

Quarter Horse Journal
P.O. Box 9105
Amarillo, TX 79105
(breed)

Quarter Horse World
P.O. Box 769
Daytona Beach, FL 32019
(breed)

Quarter Horse Youth
P.O. Box 1419
Pinehurst, NC 28374
(youth)

Rodeo News
P.O. Box 8160
Nashville, TN 37207
(rodeo)

Rodeo Sports News
2929 W. 19th Ave.
Denver, CO 80204
(rodeo)

Saddle and Bridle Magazine
2333 Brentwood Blvd.
St. Louis, MO 63144
(show)

The Trail Rider
Box 387
Chatsworth, GA 30705
(trails)

U.S. Combined Training Association
News
One Winthrop Square
Boston, MA 02110
(show)

Voice of the Tennessee Walking
Horse
P.O. Box 1117
Murfreesboro, TN 37130
(breed)

Walking Horse Report
P.O. Box 619
Shelbyville, TN 37160
(breed)

Welsh Pony World
4531 Dexter St., N.W.
Washington, D.C. 20007
(breed)

The Western Horseman
3850 N. Nevada Ave.
Colorado Springs, CO 80901
(general interest)

The Whip
King's Hill Rd.
Sharon, CT 06069
(carriages and carts)

Breed registries

American *Albino* Association, Inc.
Box 79
Crabtree, OR 97335

Andalusian Horse Registry of the
Americas
c/o Glenn Smith
P.O. Box 1290
Silver City, NM 88061

Appaloosa Horse Club, Inc.
P.O. Box 8403
Moscow, ID 83843

National *Appaloosa Pony*, Inc.
Box 297
Rochester, IN 46975

Arabian Horse Registry of America,
Inc.
One Executive Park
7801 East Belleview Ave.
Englewood, CO 80110

The *Half-Arabian* Registry and
Anglo-Arab Registry
International Arabian Horse
Association
224 East Olive Ave.
Burbank, CA 91503

American *Bashkir Curly* Registry
Box 453
Ely, NV 89301

American *Bay* Horse Registry
P.O. Box 790
Bend, OR 97701

Belgian Draft Horse Corporation of
America
P.O. Box 335
Wabash, IN 46992

American *Buckskin* Registry
Association
P.O. Box 1125
Anderson, CA 96007

International *Buckskin* Horse
Association
P.O. Box 357
St. John, IN 46373

Cleveland Bay Society of America
Berryville, VA 22611

American *Connemara Pony* Society
HoshieKon Farm
Goshen, CT 06756

American *Crossbred Pony* Registry
P.O. Box 202
Newton, NJ 07860

American *Donkey* and *Mule* Society,
Inc.
2410 Executive Dr.
Indianapolis, IN 46241

Galiceno Horse Breeders
Association, Inc.
111 E. Elm St.
Tyler, TX 75701

American *Gotland* Horse
Association
R.R. 2, Box 181
Elkland, MO 65644

American *Hackney* Horse Society
P.O. Box 174
Pittsfield, IL 62363

Horse of the Americas Registry
248 N. Main
Porterville, CA 93257

American *Indian* Horse Registry,
Inc.
Rocking LJK Ranch
Route 2, Box 127
Apache Jct., AZ 85220

Standard *Jack & Jennet* Registry of
America
Route 7 - Todds Rd.
Lexington, KY 40502

Royal International *Lipizzaner* Club
of America
Route 7
Columbia TN 38401

The American *Miniature* Horse
Registry
P.O. Box 468
Fowler, IN 47944

Missouri Fox Trotting Horse Breed
Association, Inc.
P.O. Box 637
Ava, MO 65608

Morab Horse Registry of America
P.O. Box 143
Clovis, CA 93612

American *Morgan* Horse Association
P.O. Box 265
Hamilton, NY 13346

American *Mustang* Association, Inc.
P.O. Box 338
Yucaipa, CA 92399

American *Paint* Horse Association
P.O. Box 13486
Fort Worth, TX 76118

The *Palomino* Horse Association,
Inc.
P.O. Box 324
Jefferson City, MO 65101

Palomino Horse Breeders of
America
P.O. Box 249
Mineral Wells, TX 76067

American *Part-Blooded* Horse
Registry
4120 SE River Dr.
Portland, OR 97222

American *Paso Fino* Horse
Association, Inc.
Room 3018
525 William Penn Place
Pittsburgh, PA 15219

Percheron Horse Association of
America
Route 1
Belmont, OH 43718

American Association of Owners &
Breeders of *Peruvian Paso*
Horses
P.O. Box 2035
California City, CA 94505

Peruvian Paso Half-blood Association
43058 N. 42nd St. W.
Lancaster, CA 93534

The *Pinto* Horse Association of
America, Inc.
P.O. Box 3984
San Diego, CA 92103

Pony of the Americas Club
1452 N. Federal, Box 1447
Mason City, IA 50401

American *Quarter Horse* Association
P.O. Box 200
Amarillo, TX 79168

Original *Half Quarter Horse* Registry
Hubbard, OR 97032

Standard *Quarter Horse*
4390 Fenton
Denver, CO 80212

Racking Horse Breeders of America
Helena, AL 35080

Colorado Ranger Horse Association
(*Rangerbred*)
7023 Eden Mill Rd.
Woodbine, MD 21797

American *Saddle Horse* Breeders
Association
929 South Fourth St.
Louisville, KY 40203

The *Half Saddlebred* Registry of
America
660 Poplar St.
Cochocton, OH 43812

American *Shetland Pony* Registry
P.O. Box 468
Fowler, IN 47944

American *Shire* Horse Association
Box 19
Pingree, ID 83262

Spanish-Barb Breeders Association
P.O. Box 7479
Colorado Springs, CO 80907

The *Spanish Mustang* Registry, Inc.
Route 2, Box 74
Marstall, TX 75670

The United States Trotting Association (*Standardbred*)
750 Michigan Ave.
Columbus, OH 43215

American *Suffolk* Horse Association
672 Polk Blvd.
Des Moines, IA 50312

Tennessee Walking Horse Breeders'
and Exhibitors' Association
P.O. Box 286
Lewisburg, TN 37091

The Jockey Club (*Thoroughbred*)
300 Park Ave.
New York, NY 10022

Half-Thoroughbred Registry
c/o American Remount Association,
Inc.
P.O. Box 1066
Perris, CA 92370

Trakehner Breed Association &
Registry of America, Inc.
Route 1, Box 177
Petersburg, VA 23803

American *Trakehner* Association
Norman, OK 73069

National Trotting & Pacing
Association, Inc. (*Trottingbred*)
575 Broadway
Hanover, PA 17331

New Jersey *Trotting Bred Pony*
Registry
P.O. Box 202
Newton, NJ 07860

American *Walking Pony* Association
Registry
Route 5, Box 88
Macon, GA 31201

Welsh Pony Society of America
Drawer A
White Post, VA 22663

National parks and forests with bridle trails

Note: In this listing, NP = National Park, NF = National Forest, and NM = National Monument.

For more information, consult *Horseback Vacation Guide*, by Steven D. Price, published by The Stephen Greene Press, Brattleboro, Vermont 05301.

Alaska: Chugach NF.

Arizona: Apache NF, Canyon do Chelly NM, Chiricahua NM, Coconino NF, Coronado NF, Grand Canyon NM, Grand Canyon NP, Kaibab NF, Organ Pipe Cactus NM, Prescot NF, Saguaro NM, Sitgreaves NF, Tonto NF.

Arkansas: Hot Springs NP.

California: Angeles NF, Cleveland NF, Death Valley NM, Devils Postpile NM, Eldorado NF, Inyo NF, Joshua Tree NM, Kings Canyon NP, Klamath NF, Lassen NF, Lassen Volcanic NP, Los Padres NF, Mendocino NF, Modac NF, Plumas NF, Point Reyes National Seashore, San Bernadino NF, Sequoia NF, Sequoia NP, Shasta-Trinity NF, Sierra NF, Six Rivers NF, Stanislaus NF, Tahoe NF, Yosemite NP.

Colorado: Arapaho NF, Colorado NM, Curecanti National Recreation Area, Grand Mesa-Uncompahgre NF, Gunnison NF, Mesa Verde NP, Pike NF, Rio Grande NF, Rocky Mountain NP, Roosevelt NF, Routt NF, San Isabel NF, San Juan NF, Shadow Mountain National Recreation Area, White River NF.

District of Columbia: National Capital Parks.

Georgia: Chickamauga and Chattanooga National Military Park.

Hawaii: Haleakala NP, Hawaii Volcanoes NP.

Idaho: Boise NF, Caribou NF, Challis NF, Clearwater NF, Coeur d'Alene NF, Kaniksu NF, Nez Perce NF, Payette NF, St. Joe NF, Salmon NF, Sawtooth NF, Targhee NF.

Illinois: Shawnee NF.

Maine: Acadia NP.

Maryland: Assateague Island National Seashore.

Michigan: Hiawatha NF, Huron NF, Manistee NF.

Mississippi: Bienville NF, DeSoto NF, Natchez Trace Parkway, Tombighee NF.

Missouri: Clark NF, Mark Twain NF.

Montana: Beaverhead NF, Bitteroot NF, Custer NF, Deerlodge NF, Flathead NF, Gallatin NF, Glacier NP, Helena NF, Kootenai NF, Lewis and Clark NF, Lolo NF.

Nebraska: Nebraska NF

Nevada: Humboldt NF, Toiyabe NF.

New Mexico: Bandelier NM, Carson NF, Cibola NF, Gila NF, Lincoln NF, Navajo NM, Santa Fe NF.

North Carolina: Blue Ridge Parkway.

North Dakota: Theodore Roosevelt National Memorial Park.

Oklahoma: Arbuckle National Recreation Area, Platt NP.

Oregon: Crater Lake NP, Deschutes NF, Fremont NF, Malheur NF, Mount Hood NF, Ochoco NF, Rogue River NF, Siskiyou NF, Umatilla NF, Umpqua NF, Wallowa-Whitman NF, Willamette NF, Winema NF.

South Carolina: Francis Marion NF, Sumter NF.

South Dakota: Badlands NM, Black Hills NF.

Tennessee: Great Smoky Mountains NP.

Texas: Big Bend NP.

Utah: Arches NM, Ashley NF, Bryce Canyon NP, Cache NF, Canyonlands NP, Dinosaur NM, Dixie NF, Fishlake NF, Manti-LaSal NF, Rainbow Bridge NM, Uinta NF, Wasatch NF, Zion NP.

Virginia: Jefferson NF, Shenandoah NP.

Washington: Colville NF, Coulee Dam National Recreation Area, 'ford Pinchot NF, Mount Baker NF, Mount Rainier NP, Okanogan NF, O.   ic NF, Olympic NP, Snoqualmie NF, Wenatchee NF.

Wyoming: Bighorn NF, Bridger NF, Grand Teton NP, Medicine N: Shoshone NF, Teton NF, Yellowstone NP.

Index

Acreage, amount necessary 20, 73, 106, 113, 133–34
Age, factor in choosing horse 36–38
Aids, def. 143
American Horse Council 26, 27, 138, 140, 149
American Saddle Horse 33, 143
Appaloosa 26, 143
Apples, danger of overeating 76
Arabian 26, 31, 32, 33, 143
Ascarids 78
Auction, horse 46–48; *illus. 47*

Bedding 126, 143
Belgian 33
Bibliography 146–47
Binocular vision 53–54; *illus. 53*
Bit 95–98; *illus. 96*
Blanket, using 86; *illus. 66*
Bloodworm 143
Boarding stable 15, 17–19; *illus. 19*
Bosal (hackamore) 96
Bots 78, 143
Breed(s), horse 26, 31–34
Breed organizations 136–37
Breed registries 155–58
Breeding 38
Bridle 95–96; *illus. 96*
Bridle trails 135–36, 158–59
    See also Trail-riding

Clubs, riding 13, 130–32
    See also Organizations, horsemen's

Clydesdale 33
Coggins Test 82
Colic 76, 82–83
Color, factor in choosing horse 39
Communication (horse/rider) 54–60
Community relations 17, 67–68, 104, 111, 115, 118–19, 132–34
    See also Shows, equestrian; Organizations, horsemen's
Competition, *see* Shows, equestrian
Composting 126–27
Condition, of horse 39–40, 44, 74
Conformation 31, 41–42; *illus. 43*
Cooperation, among horsemen 80–81, 129, 132, 136–38
    See also Organizations, horsemen's
Costs, *see* Expenses
County Agricultural Agent 79, 91, 109, 113–14, 118, 124, 131, 139–40

Digestion, horse 71, 74, 75–76
Disease control 81–85, 132
    See also Illness; Parasites
Disposition, of horse 31, 37–38, 40, 44, 50–51
Distemper 82
Draft horses 31, 33
Dressage 94, 144
Driving 107

Endurance riding 14
Equine infectious anemia 82, 91

Equipment 92–100, 107
See also Tack
Exercise 76–77; illus. 77
Expenses
  horse 21, 42–46
  maintenance 17–19, 21, 95, 100,
    110
  pony 34–35
  trailer 21, 100–103
Eye, see Sight

Facilities, see Feed; Pasture; Stable
Feed
  cost 21
  daily needs 72–74
  storage 108
  supplements 75
Feeding 65, 79
  facilities 111–13, 125
  overfeeding 75–76
Fences 16, 21, 106, 114–18
Fertilizer 120–21
Floating, def. 84
Fly control 124
Forests, national 136, 158–59
Founder 76
4-H horse program 131–32

Gates 16, 106, 118–19; illus. 119
Gelding, suitability of 38, 59
Grade horses 26, 33
Grain, see Feed
Grass, types 113–14
Grooming 86–88; illus. 87

Half-Arabian 26
Halter 98–99
Hand, defined 36
Hay 73–74, 75, 107, 108
Hay rack 111; illus. 112
Hazards
  to horses 110–11, 115, 116, 119
  to people 16, 35, 140–41
Health, of horse 39–40, 44, 58
  See also Illness; Parasites

Hearing, sense of 52
Height, factor in choosing horse 36
Hoof(s) 21, 88–91; illus. 89, 90
Hoof pick 88; illus. 89
Horse, historic role of 22–25;
  illus. 25
Horse clubs, see Organizations;
  Shows
Horse racing 27, 49; illus. 27
Horse Safety Guidelines 141
Horse shows, see Shows, equestrian
Horse trading 45–46
Hunting 14

Illness 75–76, 78, 81–85, 88
  See also Health; Parasites
Influenza 81–82
Injuries 85
  See also Health; Illness
Insurance
  for horses 45
  liability 16, 68, 119

Jumping 94; illus. 133

Keeneland (Lexington, Ky.) horse
  sale 48

Laminitis, see Founder
Land developments, for horsemen
  134–35
Land-use regulations 132–33
Lateral vision 53–54; illus. 53
Lead line 99–100
Liability, of horse owners 16, 68, 119
Lockjaw 81
Longe line 77; illus. 77

Magazines, horsemen's 152–55
Manure 79, 107, 125–28
Mare
  nutrition when pregnant 71
  suitability of 38, 59
Memory 37–38, 63–64
  See also Psychology; Training
Minerals 70, 72, 112–13

Morgan 33
Motivation, *see* Psychology;
   Training

Nutrition 69–77

Organizations, horsemen's 130–32,
   136–38, 147–49
Overfeeding 75–76

Palomino 145
Parasites 77–81, 83–84, 107, 126
Parks, national 136, 158–59
Pasture 21, 72–73, 79, 106–107,
   113–14, 120–22
Percheron 33
Performance
   factor in choosing horse 41–42
   specialized 30–34, 42–44
Pinworms 78–79
Poison 76, 124, 125
Pony, as alternative to horse 34–36
Popularity, horse
   current 7, 25–29
   in past 22–25
Posterior vision 53–54; *illus. 53*
Preventive medicine 83–85
Psychology, horse 37–38, 51, 57–68,
   104–105
Punishment 60–61, 63
Putting down 91

Quarter Horse 26, 31, 145

Racing, horse 27, 49; *illus. 27*
Registries, breed 26
Reward 60–62; *illus. 60*
Riding clubs, *see* Clubs
Rodent control 125
Rodeos 14, 129

Saddle 92–95; *illus. 93*
Safety 16, 100–103, 110, 140–41
Salt 70, 112–13
Saratoga Springs (N.Y.) horse sale 48
Sex, differences in horses 38

Shelter facilities, *see* Stable
Shipping fever 81–82
Shoes, for horses 21, 89–91
Shows, equestrian 13–14, 31, 94,
   102, 129–30
   See also Organizations,
   horsemen's
Sight, sense of 52–54; *illus. 53*
Size, of horses 35–36
Sleeping sickness 82
Smell, sense of 51–52; *illus. 58*
Stable 19–20, 21, 107–11, 122–25;
   illus. 109
   See also Boarding stable
Stallion, suitability of 38, 48, 59
Standardbred 33, 145
State extension specialists 150–52
State horse councils 147
Statistics, horse ownership 7, 25–27
Storage facilities 107–108
Strongyles 78
Supplements, feed 75
Swamp fever 82, 91

Tack 21, 92–100, 107; *illus. 93, 96, 99*
Teeth 47, 84
Tennessee Walking Horse 32–33
Tetanus 81
Thoroughbred 26, 31, 32, 145
Thrush 88
Trail-riding 14, 135–36
Trailer 21, 65–66, 100–103
Training
   factor in choosing horse 37–38,
   42–44, 49
   techniques for 51, 56, 59–68
Transportation, of horses 21
   See also Trailer

United States Department of
   Agriculture 139–40
Unsoundness 40, 76

Vaccinations 81–83
Veterinarian
   consultant in buying horse 40,

Veterinarian (*cont'd.*)
    47, 48, 49
    when to call 75–76, 79, 81–85, 91
Vision, *see* Sight

Washing 86–87
Water 76, 79, 113
Weed control 121
Windpuffs *illus. 84*

Worm medicine 79–80
Wrappings, protective 86; *illus. 66*
    See also Blankets

Youth activities 14, 29, 131–32
    See also Organizations,
        horsemen's

Zoning ordinances 19, 111, 132–35